The Icknield Way
Another Man following in the footsteps of Edward Thomas

John Edward

Cover design by Sorcha Edward
www.sorchaedward.com
www.thirdnightstudio.com

First Published January 2021

Copyright © John Edward 2021

johnedward.suffolk@gmail.com

ISBN:9798584925031

CONTENTS

PROLOGUE

Thomas dedicated 'The Icknield Way' to Harry Hooton. Harry Hooton was one of Thomas walking companions. He claims to have walked more miles with Harry than any other person but himself. Many of their walks together, it would seem, were along the Pilgrims Way. Thomas tangled with sections of the Pilgrims Way in the west, during his Pursuit of Spring. It is not clear from the account in the dedication if they ever walked the whole 119 miles or even, if they ever made it as far as Canterbury, however, the eighteen-mile section between Detling and Eastwell in Kent would appear to be one with which both men were familiar and Thomas reflects happily on the pubs they visited together along the way. He mentions four by name:

The Cock Horse in Detling; the Black Horse Inn in Thurnham; the Kings Head in Hollingbourne and Robert Philpot's, Woodman. This last is not marked by name on old OS maps but could have been a Beer House that is marked in an isolated terrace of cottages to the north of Lenham.

For the sake of some connection with both Pilgrims, I undertook my own pilgrimage, attempting to track down, to divine what residue of that Edwardian pastime remains. It seems likely that Thomas undertook these walks while he was living in Bearsted. Rose Acre Cottage where Thomas lived in 1901 is long gone, Ivy Cottage, where he lived until 1904 is still

1

extant. The green it faces is bookended by a choice of locals, the Bell Inn and the Oak on the Green or Royal Oak as it was then.

It is a short walk from Bearsted to Detling, though today, this requires a traverse over the M20. If they walked as far as Eastwell, it was about twenty miles and would have taken about six hours discounting the time spent in the pubs. They could have returned to Bearsted by train from either Wye or Charing Station but those kinds of details are not included in Thomas account. I stopped at Charing and returned to Bearsted by train.

Cock Horse, Detling.

[Green King IPA, Tribute, Old Speckled Hen]

From the rear, the kind of classic country pub it is easy to imagine Thomas being attracted to. Inside, it has been stripped back to the bare timber frame in keeping with modern notions of rustic charm. There is an inglenook, in places a heavily timbered ceiling, stone floor and exposed brickwork. Its rambling plan probably always presented the customer with options for both intimacy and sociability even when, as I imagine, the timber frame was hidden behind a lath and plaster coating in the early twentieth century.

It still has the feel of a pub despite the fact that in common with so many licenced premises, its food offer is to the fore.

From the front, however; a dull Green King pub. This modern 'Kentish' frontage has been imposed on the building probably since Thomas time, adding nothing to its character.

Recalling his walks with Thomas many years later, Hooton provided some insight into the kind of walking companion Thomas made:

"As we started, so for many years our ritual was unvaried. Neither intruded on the privacy of the other, neither was so silly as to point out the endless beauty of the country, we just walked in healing silence, Edwy now and then pausing to make brief notes in a pocket book...Then, in a quiet inn with a tankard of old ale [ale as it used to be]"

It suddenly becomes so much clearer just how Thomas was able to record the travels he undertook both along the Icknield Way and In Pursuit of Spring as the meditations of a man travelling alone.

Writing the dedication allowed Thomas to reflect upon the completed book. Perhaps unsurprisingly from one such as Thomas, it was not with an unbounded sense of accomplishment.

"This book for you was to have been a country book, but I see that it has turned out to be another of those books made out of books founded on other books. Being but half mine..."

Half the book was Thomas, the other half, those writers that had most influenced it. He lists the writers and the books he had used as inspiration and as reference material:

"Mr. Hilaire Belloc [Old Road], Mr. Harold T. E. Peake [chapter on prehistoric roads from memorials of old Leicestershire], and Mr. R. Hippisley Cox [Avebury]"

quoting Belloc in particular:

"The detestable habit of walking for exercise warps the soul"

Then continuing to refer to Belloc with a pointed self-criticism that could also be turned upon me,

"He condemns also men who ride along the road and into an inn yard and feel they are 'like some one in a book' this is a rather serious matter. Authors have unintentionally persuaded simple man to suffer many blisters for the chance of drinking ale in the manner of Borrow and meeting adventures."

Thomas had undertaken a considerable amount of research in preparation for his journey as the first two chapters of his book attest. In fact, these chapters comprise almost half the book by themselves. They are a difficult read for it is in chapters like them that the distance between Thomas time and the present becomes most immediate, where his rather archaic academic narrative style is most apparent and where paragraphs often run over several pages. A challenge to the modern attention span. Despite this, they reveal the dispassionate critical abilities for which he had become renowned.

Insightfully, on the subject of private research he declares:

"The danger is also in believing you have the answer to anything ..."

and with particular reference to the type of research that had begun to emerge from the eighteenth century onwards:

"...a picture of antiquarian conjecture and invention was now beginning – with exploration often of an active kind but usually kept sternly in obedience to speculation."

Unlike the pretentious assertions of the seasoned antiquarian, he concluded that his own book:

"... is about a road which begins many miles before I could come on its traces and ends miles beyond where I had to stop."

And of the roads declining importance:

"Apparently no special mediaeval use revived it throughout its course, or gave it a new entity like that of the Pilgrims' Way..."

but then:

"There is nothing at the end of any road better than maybe found beside it, though there would be no travel did men believe it."

Attempting to bring a *"little more of the mystery of the road"* into his subject, he describes the physical experience of remoteness that characterise some sections of the Way:

"...down from the realm-long bridge of islands above the world the traveller descended into cities of men"

and disarmingly:

"...ale is better than ink, though it is no substitute."

Whether or not, Harry Hooton's preference for 'Old Ale' was a reference to the kind of beer that now goes by that name, elsewhere Thomas declares a preference for Burton Ales, an altogether different brew. It is just as likely he was reminiscing about the ales they drank together before the First World War. Before they were stripped of their taste and strength by Lloyd George.

∼

B

lack Horse, Thurnham.

[Doombar, Proper Job, Long Man's Old Man]

Outwardly, a modest looking pub that Thomas would still recognise, inside it has gone through the familiar, modern transformations that so many others have in order to remain viable in a world where eking out a living from just the licencing trade alone is no longer deemed sustainable. It is now a restaurant, wedding venue and a hotel.

Many have found The Icknield Way a difficult read, the repetitive description of the route Thomas took, his description of the botanical contents of one hedgerow or verge after another or, for some relief, the description of a road with neither a hedgerow nor a verge can become monotonous and wearing. I would recommend anyone attempting it, to follow the narrative on a map.

[https://maps.nls.uk/geo/explore/#zoom=52.41540&lon=0.74739&layers =168&b=3] your starting point – search Thetford once loaded.

It is not a particularly well written book. He comes into his own in those rare moments when describing the abstract and spiritual insights the landscape moves him to express but he rarely finds the means to convey the actual essence of the landscape he is passing through in an engaging way. He rarely manages to identify its dynamic. Seebold's *Rings Around Saturn*, Robert MacFarlane's description of the Broomway in *The Old Ways*, in particular, come to mind. A little closer to Thomas time, Adrian Bell's

Men and the Fields describes a landscape peopled by those working it. Without referencing the vast array of nature writing that is now available, against these few alone, Thomas work comes a very poor second. It is not that Thomas was venturing as a pioneer of country writing for there are many passages in Hudson the *Shepherds Life* that bring the countryside to life as they describe the sweep of the landscape and the activities taking place within it and of course, the birdsong. To some extent, Thomas could be excused as he took on a format that was imposed upon him by his publisher but as country writing, both Pursuit and the Icknield Way are a step backwards from the South Country. But then, he was not only struggling with the format but with life too. The evidence of these two books, perversely, is that Thomas was not a natural country writer and it is perhaps understandable that he subsequently became better known as a poet despite this forming such a small, time limited part of his legacy.

But punctuating Thomas rather literal, one dimensional descriptions are his diversions, reveries, diatribes and fantasies. They can sometimes seem contrived, misplaced, employed just to fill a few pages with something else. They can take a bit of unravelling and sometimes provide a revealing insight into Thomas and his preoccupations and sometimes his downright cleverness. While the central theme of this book is a reflection on the changes that the past hundred years have wrought on the world Thomas travelled through, these interludes will accompany this journey too.

~

Kings Head, Hollingbourne.

[Harvey's Best Bitter, Musket Brewery's Trigger, Doombar]

All the street presence of a classic English Inn, rather disappointingly, it now goes by the name, 'The Dirty Habit' and treads that narrow path between its history and the demands of the modern age.

The Pilgrims Way, as Thomas stated in the dedication, was given *"a new entity"* and is now, formally, a long-distance footpath. This is not the case with the Icknield Way for there is one important distinction about the Icknield Way that must be made. The Icknield Way Path and the Icknield Way are two distinctly different routes. The Icknield Way Path is a modern contrivance that attempts to plot a route through the countryside conducive to the walker. It does not follow the same route as the Icknield Way, often deviating from it to avoid the places that have become compromised in the modern age. It is, like most modern long-distance footpaths, based on some kind of conjecture and invention but kept sternly in obedience to convenience. The narrative in this book relates only to the route Thomas followed, that is the historic Icknield Way.

The Pilgrims Way is a single tracked, blacktop road from Detling to Hollingbourne. The North Downs, rising on the left is reminiscent of the later sections of the Icknield Way itself. Beyond the King's Head it reverts to an unmetalled track but its surface, mangled by 4x4's and motorbikes, has been worn into deep ruts that have left an unpleasant surface for a walker. Perhaps this mangling is not an altogether a modern phenomenon but was preceded by the mauling it received under the wheels of the horse and cart in Edwardian times and earlier. For the rest of the Way, it is a mixture of track with an unpleasant friable surface interspersed with short sections of blacktop. I could say that either its condition was different in Edwardian times or we have become soft. Expecting the Way to be prepared for us, to be managed by...someone. What seems more likely is that attempts to maintain the track against the onslaught of modern foot and wheeled traffic have caused the administrators to import large quantities of road stone. This road stone is not of consistent quality and can vary in grade between a gravel-like aggregate to something more the size of house bricks. The result, to me, is a surface that is unsuitable to any, least of all and Edwardian not equipped with modern walking boots.

~

The Woodman, Maybe.

The old map indicates a beerhouse in this end of terrace of cottage just to the north of Lenham and a short distance from the Way. Thomas direct reference to 'Robert Philpot' suggests he and Harry may have had a particularly personal relationship with this establishment and gives additional support to the Woodman being a beerhouse rather than a pub. It is only speculation. I have been unable to find any references to a 'Woodman' or a 'Robert Philpot' anywhere between here and Canterbury. The nearest equivalent to a beerhouse in the modern age is perhaps the Micro Pub. There is one in Charing, my next and final destination.

~

The Bookmakers Arms, Charing.

[Crispin Amber, Mad Cats Jester Pale, Curious Brew]

Like the personal reference to Robert Philpot, the modern micropub is a thing apart from the mainstream pub. They are generally an altogether more intimate experience and the Bookmakers Arms is no exception. Established in an old shop, like all micropubs, the landlord takes an interest in the beers purveyed in a way the Pubco never will, offering diversions rather more creative than the additional income stream provided by the jukebox and gaming machines. Sure, not all well run pubs are micropubs, but as we have seen along the Pilgrims Way, many have had to diversify into the food and boutique accommodation trade.

It is hard to visualise Thomas world accurately, so much has changed. Change that cannot be fathomed by a survey of the remaining artefacts alone. In some towns, we can catch a glimpse of the world he lived in. For instance, those with Late Victorian and Edwardian town extensions that gathered around the historic cores. His disdain for the growth of the suburbs is more confidently stated in his later book, In Pursuit of Spring and perhaps the less urban character of this journey did not bring the issue into such a sharp focus, however, glimpses of his discontent are present.

There are passages in Thomas other country writings where he seems to attempt to capture the essence of a deep communion with nature and his place within it. His acquiescence to his publisher's suggestion that he name the places he passed through in this book is one insight into the change in

11

the dynamic of the narrative but not a complete explanation. It is not as if he ever stopped walking, but it came at a time when he was struggling with his mental health. I would speculate that the need to walk was strongest in him when in the depths of his melancholy. In his attempts to fathom the answers to his pain against the backdrop of his virtually godless universe.

Moments of deep communion in this book are as rare for Thomas as they are for most people, for the minds unremitting chatter of distraction is always present.

In undertaking such a journey now, the even greater gulf between us and the possibility of uninterrupted deep immersion is obvious, overlaid as it is with so many additional layers of distraction. But for Thomas, even when attempting to be fully immersed, travelling like Belloc or like Borrow, he seems to achieve this at best, only fleetingly.

In his book *The Old Road*, Belloc got close to describing in simple language the virtually unbridgeable gulf between the civilised mind and the primordial mind:

 "...before we were quite men we knew it, for the animals still have it today; they seek their food and their drinking-places, and, as I believe, their assemblies, by known tracks which they have made."

Thomas expressed it more abstractly, capturing it best in his references to birds and to name the most obvious, notably in the last stanza of Adlesdrop.

The roadside plants might now have to absorb the toxins spread amongst them by the internal combustion engine, the birdsong, drowned out by traffic, the distant views often obscured by unmaintained hedgerow. Modern development is of a different order again. Modern dentistry, antibiotics, CAT scanners, the NHS, slum clearance, unemployment benefit are often cited as some of the more desirable advances of the modern age. It would be interesting to know what Thomas would have traded for the modern world.

I would trade Thatcher for one experience of the lost pubs he passed but such a win win is no trade at all. We would be deluding ourselves to imagine that Thomas would not have similarly traded her for a world that turned in a different direction too.

I cannot say I shared this journey with Thomas but in retrospect, there were experiences running in parallel. There were certain unplanned things that gathered my attention progressively as the journey proceeded. As Thomas must also have known, they continue to work on you long after the physical journey itself is complete.

CHAPTER 1
FIRST DAY — THETFORD TO NEWMARKET, BY LACKFORD AND KENTFORD

A brief description of today's route:

On day one, Thomas travelled about twenty miles. As far as Lackford, this was on off road trackways. They have not changed dramatically in character since his journey in 1911. Between Lackford and Kentford, the route Thomas travelled is now, in the main, a relatively quiet C Class road. Beyond Kentford a modern B Class road takes the route to Newmarket. When Thomas used this road, it would have been the main route into Newmarket and beyond from the east, before the bypass was constructed.

***

Thomas journeyed to Thetford by train. He opens his narrative with an account of a rather one-way conversation with a:

"... a vast handsome fellow nearing sixty, well bearded, whiskered, and moustached, but not so as to hide full red lips and small, cheerful, and penetrating dark eyes..."

...who provided Thomas with an opinion on many things, the particulars of his large family and a verdict on Thomas planned walking tour of the Icknield Way.

"As he perceived that I was not in business he assumed that I was taking a dose of walking, one of the most expensive medicines, and, as he believed, one of the best"

From the station, Thomas headed towards the Castle, a route that would have taken him through the centre of a town which he considered:

"...a most pleasant ancient town, built of flints, full of turns and comers and yards. It smelt of lime trees and of brewing."

Thetford was a respectably sized market town in 1911, the smell of brewing would have come from Bidwells Brewery in Old Market Street. Despite its remoteness from the coast, Thetford became Walmington on Sea in the Dad's Army TV series. In real life, it was the birthplace of Thomas Paine.

The Little Ouse sweeps in from the south wrapping around the castle mound joining the River Thet as it, in turn, wraps around from the north. Conjoined, they head west. On the map of the town, the castle sits in this confluence like an Egyptian eye. The London Road, like a seven-mile-long spear from the southwest skewers the heart of the town centre. The river sweeps further west then north through its flood plain. Always mimicking the river but on the north side of the town, the railway once swept down like a sinewave from the north and wrapped around the town and castle then headed away to Bury in the south after peeling off at the crest of the intersection of the two waves to Attleborough and Watton along what was then the Great Eastern Railway. Watton and Bury were excommunicated by Beeching. The A1066 town bypass opportunistically follows the line of the old Bury branch line taking traffic away from the town centre to Diss in the east and Ixworth in the southeast along the A1088. Development now spreads far beyond the edges of the town that Thomas would have seen. Towards the north and east absorbing the London 'overspill' in the post-war years. The A11, once, in parts the Icknield Way, now bypasses the town to the west and seems, so far, to be the ring-pass-not to all development to the west and south.

According to the old map, the great expanses of the Thetford Forest plantations had already begun in earnest in Thomas time. Radiating out ten miles from the town centre in an arc to the north and west. We all too often attribute this kind of planting to modern times but as this record attests, it clearly predated the Forestry Commission.

Thomas began his commentary on the Way itself next to the castle and speculated that the Icknield Way came into Thetford from the northeast along the line of a greenway which crosses the railway before connecting with Castle Lane. The greenway now bisects a large modern housing area. Though Thetford has seen considerable development in the post-war years the picturesque charm of flint faced buildings and the narrow lanes that attracted Thomas attention still characterise much of Thetford's central core.

Thomas headed into the eastern side of the town centre where he encountered his first pub.

"I noticed on the right hand a very strange fish on a signboard, a very curly fish, with curly whiskers, three curled plumes on his back, and a curled tail"

In the early stages of researching Thomas book, this pub seemed like the ideal starting point. It could only have been in the few weeks before my visit that it closed. Whatever it was called in Thomas time, the aquatic theme had been maintained. A typical Thetford brick, clunch and flint building in Old Market Street. According to the large numerals built into its façade, it dates from 1624. It last traded as the Dolphin. I clicked onto the web address of the pub seeking news of its fate and was redirected to an American website attempting to sell its domain name for $2,000. Just how out of time is this with Thomas own. I had to find another pub and without too much deliberation chose the Albion.

The Albion. Thetford.

[IPA, Abbot, Woodfords Werry]

Clean, unglamorous, keeping a range of real ales, it is busy with banter and good humour. I see no reason why Thomas would not have felt comfortable here, sitting quietly in the corner taking in the surroundings anonymously, just as I am now.

The illustrations by A.L. Collins, which punctuated the original book come in two forms. 51 pencil sketches and 8 full-colour illustrations. In some cases, they are randomly distributed in the book. Sometimes out of sequence and sometimes detached from the narrative that describes the physical location. I have included them as close to Thomas descriptions as my own narrative and typesetting skills will allow. The pencil illustrations, particularly, have been taken from photographs if not traced directly. These photos seem to have been taken in early spring or in the winter as the trees captured in them are bare.

Following the recent discovery of the photographs Thomas took on his

Pursuit of Spring two years later, it would be brilliant if copies of the photos on which these illustrations were based were similarly discovered, buried in one of Thomas archives. More likely, they have been cleared out of an Edwardian professional photographers studio decades ago, or maybe they still reside in the archive of Constable & Co. Ltd or their successors. A research project awaits someone.

Unlike the photos taken by Thomas during his Pursuit of Spring, the location of the illustrations in The Icknield Way are generally clearly referenced. I have attempted to replicate the original photos as accurately as my limited photographic skills and the changes in the physical geography will allow.

~

The Albion faces the Castle, close to the site of the first illustration in the book. *'Castle Hill, Thetford'*

It is a view of the castle mound from the south-east near Castle Lane, looking north-west. The scene has not changed dramatically. To control erosion, a flight of steps giving access to the summit is a rather ugly intrusion. Of the two young trees at the foot of the mound in the illustration, one has grown to full maturity. The rather fanciful bucolic rendering Collins has given this image is now most definitely parkland maintained by mowers rather than sheep.

Thomas left the town heading south, initially across the River Thet then west past an old nunnery and the workhouse. The visual tranquillity of the riverside landscape around the Nun's Bridges is now shattered by a continual stream of cars and vans waiting in sequence to cross the single carriageway bridges. The remnants of the nunnery have been preserved but the workhouse Thomas remarked on as he passed it has given way to housing. Thomas briefly touched London Road as he left the town but took a track on the left towards Elveden Hall about a mile and half further on. At this point, he left Norfolk and entered Suffolk. This led him onto what is now a C Class road and then a track that is named the Icknield Way on both the old map and modern maps and is coincident at this point with both the

'Angles Way' and 'St. Edmunds Way'. From here, then and now, it is an open countryside traversed by several miles of track before the next settlement.

There are some particularly long sections of Thomas route that pass through little but open countryside, punctuated by the occasional barn but few settlements. The first section of the walk from Thetford is a case in point and as Thomas observes:

"On the ten miles between Thetford and Mildenhall there is nothing but Elveden Church, motor-cars, milestones, and dust"

It is a remorselessly flat, sandy landscape of woodland, dry heath like plains where not cultivated but enlivened by the gloriously magical scots pine windbreaks, like an Arthur Rackham elven procession that animate this Breckland landscape.

Beyond Elveden Hall, the track enters and passes through the King's Forest for much of the way to Lackford. When Thomas passed this way, many of the nursery planting belts which gave structure to the forest were already well established and as he observed:

"The sun blazed from the sky overhead and the sand underfoot; it burnt the scent out of the pines as in an oven; it made the land still and silent; but it wrenched no word or thought of blasphemy out of me. On the other hand, I felt no benevolence towards the planters of trees in straight lines; for by doing this they had destroyed the possible sublimity of this sandy land, and at the same time increased its desolation by the contrasting verdure of verdure and the obviously utilitarian arrangement."

This is still a quiet landscape, perhaps more so now than when Thomas passed this way. The King's Forest has become a uniform coniferous plantation, deep and long and silent. In an area noted for the stone curlew and the woodlark, there must be roe deer and muntjac's roaming these parts too but they are shy creatures. In this manufactured woodland it is as if, rather than shyness, the wildlife has rejected our creation. It is a lonely walk through this dark canopy, an unsettling reminder of loss.

Just beyond the edge of the King's Forest, Thomas crossed the River Lark towards Lackford and the site of the second illustration. *'Bridge and Ford, Lackford'*.

The brick bridge that carried the track has gone. The route that crosses the river has now been diverted onto the A1101. A modern steel and concrete bridge carries the A1101 across the river a few yards further downstream from the original.

Lackford

"Lackford is a village that straggles along a mile of road with such intervals of verdure that I thought I was past the end of it when I came to where I could get tea."

It still straggles along the road but in a more late-20th Century way. Intermediate sites have been infilled and a typically clumsy village extension of mid-20th Century semi-detached, detached and chalet bungalows have been added to the north. As the village blog strapline says, *'Life, but not as you know it...'* well I have to disagree. This is exactly what it looks like in all too many places now. The village extension aside, it is little more than the hamlet it was in Thomas time and there is little in the way of facilities. A church, a bus stop and a place where the post office used to be. It is very close to West Stow which Thomas describes as a *"...place where Anglo-Saxon coins, weapons, and arms have been found"* and where there is now a partial reconstruction of an Anglo Saxon Village with more visitor facilities than were ever available in Lackford.

"There was no inn; but the shop was better than the inn could have been. My hostess was one of those most active, little, stoutish and cheerful women who never go out if they can help it. Being descended from suffering and sometimes roofless generations, they seem to see no reason for returning to inclement nature when they have a good digestion and a water-tight roof; they make good jam and good tea"

One of the unmistakable features of In Pursuit of Spring was Thomas sympathies for travelling people. His sympathies may have been based on the romanticism of Borrow to some extent but they are still his. Such references are fewer and further between in The Icknield Way but here, this is the first passing declaration.

Thomas retraced his steps back through the village and re-joined the Way a little to the north, heading almost due west. From here Thomas embarked on a five-mile long trek across the Breckland countryside towards Kentford on what was then *"...an ordinary white road between hedges"*. It is now a fully metaled C Class road with a blacktopping. He describes passing a mixture of heathland, arable land, woodland and pine plantations. On route, he passed near Cavenham where the Way was carried on a new bridge next to the remains of an old brick bridge. This is the third illustration, *'Near Cavenham'*.

It is a view back along the Way towards Lackford. This characteristic of the illustrations, taking a view back along the Way rather than forward, while not universal is typical of many of the illustrations in the book.

Remarkably and perhaps as an indicator of the extent of change in the countryside in the past 100 years hereabouts, the view is practically unchanged. The road now has a blacktop surface, the telegraph now passes through the scene and as in so many other places, verdure closes off the views of the otherwise open countryside. Perhaps more disturbingly, the ditch was dry during my visit, whereas Collins illustration suggests a healthy flow of water under the bridge. However, such illusions of an unchanged countryside do not last long in the modern world.

For here, we leave the relatively tranquil tracks through the Brecks and join the modern world. Just beyond Slade Bottom where the track passes under the railway, the A14 dual carriageway crashes through, severing the link with both the old Bury Road that Thomas would have used to approach Kentford and his own experience of this place. The route is now diverted around the slip road then on to the B1506.

Kentford

Kentford, though small, is the first settlement since Thetford which seems something more than a backwater.

The old map names three pubs, the Old Cock, the Fox and Ball and the Bell. Thomas lists only the Old Cock and the Fox and Ball. The Old Cock has become The Kentford, the Fox and Ball has been converted into three cottages – Fox House, Golden Cottage and Ball Cottage. The Bell, a 16th-century coach house at the western edge of the village still trades. The old map shows Regal Lodge just behind the Old Cock which would have been Lillie Langty's home when Thomas passed this way. Thomas has much to say about advertising and the dubious claims of the virtue attached to many of the products in some of his other works. Here was one who was well ahead of the modern game, becoming not only a professional beauty but an endorser of a range of beauty products.

The Kentford or The Old Cock, Kentford.

[IPA, Speckled Hen and Abbott]

A distinctive bar, the high, deeply coved ceiling lending it a barn like quality. A six-foot high wainscot is in scale with the voluminous interior. Painted matt black with deep red paintwork above, it adds to the drama. Its boarded floor, eclectic mix of vintage and upscaled industrial furniture and a large ornate chandelier hanging in the middle of the room completes the singular style that has been brought to this pub. Madonna performs on the TV over the fireplace. It is tuned into Magic TV. A small ante-room off the bar is furnished with a bookshelf stacked with books and games for the diversion of the customers. There is a nice garden out back too.

The landlord or manager is on edge, nervously flitting around the bar area, backwards and forwards between the bar and the restaurant next door while the female bar worker serves me. What is the source of his nervousness. I am unable to divine. Life in general. Do I approve or am I showing disdain for the unusual décor. Will I be the last customer today. Will I spend enough money to cover the wear and tear on the door hinges as I entered the establishment, the upholstery, the glassware. Has a customer sneaked into the restaurant while his attention has been distracted by me. Meanwhile, Madonna displays her carefully choreographed self-assurance as if in rebuke.

Invention and authenticity and what we take for real.

The bar is in an extension to the original building. It would not have been here when Thomas passed this way. The bar he would have known is now the restaurant.

By contrast to the route Thomas took in 'In Pursuit of Spring' where he was mainly following established roads, it is in the nature of a path such as the Icknield Way, a path that is so closely associated with antiquity rather than the needs of even the medieval traveller that many sections of it have remained just a track. Or is that so. Is the Icknield way anything more than a phantom, a modern age conceit. Thomas seems to have spent a considerable time researching the Icknield Way in the British Museum. From his account, there are many but really no more than tantalising references to the antiquity of the Icknield Way going back to the seventeenth century and before. These references and in some cases, maps, created by other antiquarian researchers, have attempted to establish the authenticity of what has often been considered one of many trackways established by the 'Ancient Britons'. The contradictions between the numerous 'original sources' kept the conjecture surrounding its origins and route open for generations. And as Thomas wryly observed:

"...a picture of antiquarian conjecture and invention [emerged]....with exploration often of an active kind usually kept sternly in obedience to

speculation".

Much of Thomas research appears to have been original and his account of it shows his finely tuned and it would seem objective critical abilities at work. There is little evidence that his conclusions were in anyway framed *"...sternly in obedience to speculation".* What is evident is that for centuries there has been a will to establish the credibility of the conjecture. By the time Thomas undertook his journey some form of consensus had already formed and the OS maps of the time named most of the route Thomas followed as the Icknield Way in Gothic Lettering and as he observes:

> *"...some Berkshire people even call the Ridgeway the Icknield Way because it is the Government name... attached with all the honour of Old English lettering"*

This practise continues in modern mapping so who can realistically question the authenticity of these clearly established facts. Having read Thomas account in Chapter 2 of the Icknield Way, I am inclined to think that substance has been conjured out of the vapours through the repartition of conjecture down the ages. How easily everyday consciousness is conditioned by familiarity and sanctioned authority. It follows that much of the modern conjecture about our origins and our glories is built on a house of cards.

~

Kentford is the location of the next illustration, No.4: *'Kentford'.* It shows the ford next to the bridge over the River Kennett.

On the right of the illustration are the gnarled remains of the buttresses of an older bridge. The construction of a modern bridge has made the ford and the remains of the older bridge inaccessible in the way they were in Thomas time. Consequently, the illustration cannot be replicated accurately.

Beyond the bridge were three terraces of cottages. The first and the third pair of cottages are still there. The first pair is now obscured by roadside verdure in the photo. The thatched pair between them have made way for a new access to a modern backland development behind the remaining cottages. The third pair, with the loft window in the gable, the only ones now visible from this location.

There is a four-mile stretch of road between Lackford and Newmarket that runs fairly straight. Somewhere along this four-mile stretch of road is the site of the next illustration, No5: *'The Icknield Way and old parallel tracks near Newmarket'*.

The deep grass margin to the left of the B1506 hint at the location of the *'old parallel track'*. The telegraph posts are long gone and the rutted tracks lost in the encroaching roadside verdure and transformed into an unremarkable verge.

From Well Bottom the hedgerow and grass margins on each side of the road become heavily managed, the grass margins mown and the hedges neatly clipped to a uniform height with the roadside faces raking back from the vertical at an angle of about eighty degrees and it continues this way for over a mile until the junction with the A1304 on the outskirts of the town. The hedges have something of National Hunt Racing about them. Odd for a flat racing town like Newmarket. However, the hedges eventually give way to open views of the gallops on the final approach and an avenue of lime trees that lead into the town centre. They look too young to have been growing here when Thomas walked this way.

Newmarket

Newmarket is in a bubble of Suffolk that protrudes into Cambridgeshire, the neck of this bubble on the approach to Newmarket is a mere 100 metres across. From this point, it balloons out to encompass the whole town.

The town centre still starts with a 5-way junction as it did when Thomas passed this way. Then it wrapped around the Jubilee Clock which forms a focal point of the vista on the approach to the town from the west. The junction has now been reengineered into a roundabout to the right of the clock tower. The surrounding gallops have kept this approach to the town clear from development. Most of the expansion of the town is to the north filling in the space between the High Street and the A14 bypass that now wraps around its northern edge.

The High Street is the location of the sixth illustration, *'Newmarket'*.

Despite the redevelopment of many buildings, the character of the High Street is remarkably like the one Thomas would have seen, superficially at least. There are modern intrusions that have disrupted the otherwise uniform street frontage here and there. Many of the all too familiar clone town brands that occupy most modern high streets are present but the pubs, hotels and the Jockey Club still add their more traditional character.

The site of the illustration is from the pavement on the south side of the street looking back to the east with the Jubilee Clock Tower terminating the view. The Bull can be seen at the extreme left of the frame, the profile of the roofline and especially the chimneys are in many cases unchanged, even the scale of the shop fronts does not look dramatically different. The blacktop road surface, the parked cars and the style of dress the more obvious differences. In the illustration at least, there is that same busyness about the place.

This is where Thomas spent his first evening but his take on the place is altogether different from either the illustration or the modern scene.

"As I came into Newmarket before dark, but after the closing of shops, the long wide street and a strange breed of men standing or slowly walking about on its pavements made me feel that scarcely after a dozen reincarnations should I enter Newmarket and be at home. The man who discovered that we are 'all God's creatures' had an uncanny eye for resemblance, and I often doubt the use of the discovery, without disputing its accuracy."

On the basis of this observation Thomas embarks on a diatribe distancing himself from the racing fraternity, temperance, golfers and motorists in equal measure. This diatribe is perhaps the least emotionally complex, the most innocent. It reflects an uncomplicated enthusiasm through which he expressed his thoughts on the satisfactory completion of his first day. It does not last.

The sport of kings resulted in a town that in 1911 had at least six substantial hotels according to the old map. Thomas sought somewhere rather more modest but typically obtuse about his overnight accommodation he only reveals that:

"A Scotch baker directed me to a place — 'It is not very elaborate, but it is clean' — where I could get a bed such as I could afford."

Perhaps against his more natural disdain, Thomas let his imagination drift away into an end of day reverie led by the sound of the motorised traffic passing through the town that evening. We may take it for granted today but in 1911, the sound of motorised traffic was still quite new, still mixed with the sounds of horse drawn vehicles. The *"...wordless music of mystery and adventure"* they invoked, led him towards sleep within half an hour.

The Bull, Newmarket.

Thomas names none of the town's pubs or hotels, though according to the old map, there were many.

The Waggon and Horses, the Golden Lion and the Bull are in a row in the High Street. I chose the Bull for the robustness of this classic pub name. A dark, heavily timbered, almost maze like interior supported here and there with cast iron posts where walls have been removed. It is serving IPA and Holy Grail, a contradiction in terms.

Dark oak panelled walls in places, elsewhere wainscot, a '60's wood block floor and traditional dark wood pub furniture. Racing memorabilia adorns the walls. Some of *"God's creatures"*, that *"strange breed of men"* sat about the place in groups glued to any one of the several tv screens showing Racing TV from Redcar whispering tipsters' incantations in Pigeon Inglish as a stranger passes too close by. There is a distinctive smell of tobacco about the place, allowances are made on the non-conformist edges of the Sport of Kings. A large but empty outdoor space suggests this place expects to be packed on race days. Whether these people represent the racing fraternity or just punters I am just not familiar enough with this culture to judge. The Rutland Hotel opposite, I presume, is the domain of the racehorse owners. Another, another world within the king's strict hierarchy. This not a pub I could warm to but it represents that aspect of Newmarket well. Though Thomas enjoyed watching the horses as he left the town, I doubt that the Rutland Hotel or the Bull was his kind of place either.

CHAPTER 2
SECOND DAY — NEWMARKET TO ODSEY, BY ICKLETON AND ROYSTON

A brief description of the route:

On day two, Thomas travelled about 30 miles. He left Newmarket heading west on what is now a B Class road. The character of this road would have been fairly consistent as far as Ickleton. Now, apart from the first few miles outside Newmarket, it is a dual carriageway and a dispiriting route for anything but motorised transport and even for that, unmemorable. From Ickleton, the Way returns to some semblance of the tracks Thomas used interspersed with sections of C Class roads until just outside Royston where it joins the A505 just before entering the town. Beyond Royston, we are back on a dual carriageway again that flashes past Thomas destination for the day.

***

Thomas overnight accommodation in Newmarket cost him just 2/- though it probably did not include the cost of a supper or a breakfast. Two years later Thomas was typically paying in the region of four shillings for his overnight accommodation when he undertook his Pursuit of Spring though this sum usually included either a supper or a breakfast. This was not a period of rampant inflation, perhaps more a reflection of what he thought he could afford at that time.

The mown grass verges and neatly clipped hedges that now carry the road into Newmarket are replicated on the road out of the town. The Suffolk and Cambridgeshire borders join the road for about a mile and a half, to the point where the Devils Ditch earthwork crosses the road. Here, the Suffolk bubble bursts as Thomas entered Cambridgeshire. This is the site of the seventh illustration, *'Devil's Ditch'*.

It looks north along the dyke with the racecourse buildings in the middle distance.

Although the telegraph posts have gone, shrubs and trees have since invaded the dyke at its margins cutting off the views of the more distant landscape towards the Cambridgeshire Fens. Modern racecourse buildings replace those in the illustration.

The mown margins and hedges of the A1304 give way first to ranch style fences, then woodland before opening up again to the north to the wide-open skies and vistas across the plains of Cambridgeshire. The road beyond Newmarket runs straight and flat for six miles. This kind of terrain is challenging for most, even a seasoned walker like Thomas, so:

"...it was not long before I began to look out for a cart to carry me over the next six miles of the straight road. Such a road is tiring, because either

the eye or the mind's eye sees long, taunting, or menacing lengths before it, and is brought into conflict with sheer distance..."

At Six Mile Bottom, which unsurprisingly, is approximately six miles from Newmarket, Thomas would have passed the Green Man on the junction of the Wilbraham Road. It traded up until about 2016 but is now closed. Thomas did not mention it. In the early part of the journey, Thomas mentions few of the pubs he passes, in fact, he passes few pubs but as the journey proceeded, it is as if he began to take more notice of their waymarking function. Much later in the journey there comes a point when he fails to mention all but a few that he passes. It is a discipline that he carried over into his Pursuit of Spring, there enthusiastically, right from the start. Just after Six Mile Bottom the road crosses the railway and veers round to the southwest as it re-joins the A11. Between here and Ickleton the A11 has been reconstructed as a dual carriageway complete with slip roads, flyovers and underpasses till it merges with the M11. The road engineering might be quite different but the landscape remains the same as far as Stumps Cross. It is just hidden from the road by the modern roadside planting zones.

The road bisects another dyke, Fleam Dyke, the site of the eighth illustration, *'Fleam Dyke'*. Thomas would have simply seen the dyke stretching away from the road to the north and to the south. That is no longer possible. It is screened from the road by a close boarded fence to the south and trees to the north. In his typically cynical way Thomas commented:

"On my right was an artificial wall of turf going in the same direction as the road. This might have been an ancient earthwork, if the map had not said 'Old Railway.' A disused railway embankment gave me more pleasure than a prehistoric dyke."

As he approached Fleam Dyke Thomas could see the chimneys of Cambridge six miles distant. This was commonplace during the industrial period. Even modestly sized towns signalled their location in the landscape in this way. Fred Dibner played his part in erasing these once commonplace features from the post-industrial landscape.

The dyke is all but invisible from the dual carriageway and a visit to the site of the illustration now requires a lengthy diversion along country lanes, then a footpath and back along the dyke itself from the south.

Fleam Dyke is the second of a series of four dykes that controlled passage along the Icknield Way and is the last one to be illustrated in the book. They are considered to be Saxon, rather than prehistoric or Iron Age in origin and were upgraded over a period of a couple of centuries, from the fifth through to the seventh century. Fleam Dyke stretched as far as what were the fens to the north and a densely wooded countryside to the south. It provided a checkpoint rather than an impenetrable barrier as it could easily have been circumvented through either the fens or the woodland albeit via a long diversion through a less hospitable countryside.

The illustration is to the south, taken a little way down the side of the embankment. This is no longer possible as the whole dyke has been invaded with a dense thicket of thistle, elder, thorn, dog rose and other shrubs I do not have the skill to identify. One wonders who or what kept the dyke clear for the twelve hundred or so years up until Thomas time and what change in management has resulted in it becoming so overgrown in the last hundred. The answer is on a nearby interpretation board. The dyke was grazed by sheep up until the 1940's.

Just before what is now the Abingdon Science Park, Thomas would have crossed over the Cambridge, Haverhill and Sudbury Branch Line passing within sight of Pampisford Station with its Railway Inn. The line of the railway is now just another earthwork like the one Thomas admired next to Fleam Dyke. The station and the pub lay under the A11 and A 505 interchange.

A little beyond the interchange, Brent Ditch, the third Saxon dyke crosses the road. Thomas gives it only a passing reference.

This section of road to Ickleton is also indicated on both the old and modern maps as the line of a Roman Road. Halfway along this stretch, it is joined by the Essex border which follows Thomas route to the edge of Ickleton.

Ickleton

Thomas entered Ickleton from Stumps Cross along a lane, forded the River Cam, crossed the Great Eastern Railway and arrived in the village almost opposite the church. A traverse across the M11 is now required to gain access to this path from the north. Otherwise, traffic is diverted along the A1301 from the Stumps Cross interchange, through Hixton then back south towards Ickleton. There is one illustration of Ickleton, No 9: 'Ickleton'. It looks west along Abbey Street near the Ickleton Lion.

The single and the two-storey buildings in the foreground of the illustration have been demolished and replaced by a grim pair of bungalows. Rather surprisingly in this age of loft conversions, the terrace of thatched cottages have lost their dormers. Apart from the blacktop road and footpaths, the clutter of parked cars and the absence of children playing in the street, there are few other significant changes in this view today and yet it is as if from another world.

Of the village more generally, it has barely changed in size. Some of the open spaces have been infilled with later post-war development. There is still much flint as Thomas noted, a lot of rendered buildings, some with low key pargeting but much less thatch. It retains a quaintness without quite being picturesque. Some of this visual erosion is due to the more recent brick buildings that have replaced older ones or infilled the spaces between them. The old map shows two pubs, one named the Duke of Wellington Inn. It was not mentioned by Thomas and closed in 1957. Facing the church across a small triangular green, it is now a house. In fact, Thomas added none of the pubs in this village to his inventory. The other unnamed pub on Thomas route through the village is the Lion, now The Ickleton Lion. There were several other pubs off Thomas route but this is the only one that still trades. The village was once graced by the White Horse and the Headless Duck in Abbey Street, the New Inn in Brookhampton Street, the Beehive beerhouse in Frogge Street and the Jolly Butcher. Another world indeed.

ckleton Lion, Ickleton.

[Old Golden Hen, Timothy Taylor, IPA]

A timber-framed building with a boarded floor and painted wainscot, it is furnished with upholstered drum seats. The colour scheme now follows the well worn gastro pallet of warm neutral colours though there is no food today. As I take my seat, I am presented with a complimentary glass dish of peanuts. A nice touch. I presume, perhaps incorrectly, that Thomas would have disapproved of the background music, been surprised by the number of young children inside the pub, found the beer rather weak and as for that lager stuff! An old sepia photo of an Edwardian cycling club on the wall would at least provide him with one point of contact with the world as he saw it and inspiration for his next journey.

Despite their questionable origins, real or imagined, something about these ancient ways resonates in the psyche. There is a genuine allure in these high-level trackways.

It might be hard to recognise this in the flatlands of East Anglia that Thomas had just passed through, though in the remoter parts, even here there is an otherworldliness at times. In the section of the Upper Icknield Way that is yet to come, this sense of passing across an undulating landscape between a series of islands takes much less of a leap of the imagination. There are long sections that pass through no settlements. The only way to reconnect with the world of man on these paths is either to follow them till their end or to take a diversion down *"into the cities of men"*.

There is little doubt that these trackways exist and are ancient, it is more a case of, was there once a coherent route across the country that was called the Icknield Way or more rather, a series of local routes upon which this concept has been laid in later times. As Thomas states elsewhere in the introductory chapters following both his studies in the British Library and the fieldwork he undertook during his journey:

"*I could not find a beginning or an end of the Icknield Way. It is thus a symbol of mortal things with their beginnings and ends always in immortal darkness.*"

Thomas does not censor his own speculations; however, he ensures that they are not framed *"sternly in obedience"* to them. Here in Ickleton, he was touching the edge of Capricorn in the Nuthampstead Zodiac. I would not make too much of these correspondences though they are in some way compatible with the mystery and allure of the Icknield Way itself.

~

Thomas left Ickleton along Abbey Street and onto trackways for several miles. The Icknield Way follows Grange Road as it passes over the M11, now on the very edge of Ickleton, divides at a fork and continues past Ickleton Grange through an arable countryside. At Ickleton Grange it turns to the north, picks up the line of the Hertfordshire Cambridgeshire border which it follows after a turn back to the west then shortly after, leaves both at a 'T' junction with another C Class road and follows an unmetalled track beyond heading almost due west.

After the miles of dual carriageway leading up to Ickleton and despite the proximity of the M11, something in the character of the environment the Way now passes through; the hush, the way it seems to meld back into a more timeless landscape; suggests a prelude.

Somewhere along these tracks, Thomas narrative records an encounter with an unusual woman.

"A huge wheel and windlass and a seven-gallon tub stood above a well in the yard. A wild-looking cat bounded through the window of one of the cottages which seemed to be empty..... She was a thin, hawk- faced woman, bare and brown to the breast, and with glittering blue eyes, and in her upper jaw three strong teeth. She was dressed in black rags. She shaded her eyes to look at me, as if I were half a mile away."

Thomas records a rather surreal conversation, real or imagined.

"You're thin boy" she said, *"like me"*
"Yes."
A pause.
"Are you middling well off?"
"Yes, middling. Are you?"
"Oh, middling; but times are hard."
"They are."
She looked extraordinarily sad, and I said: —
"Still, we shall have a few years to wait for the workhouse."
"Have to wait a few years!"
she repeated, very serious, though smiling.
"Have you come from Royston?"
"No; Newmarket."
"Newmarket. Are you going far?"
"To Odsey, between Royston and Baldock"
"It's a long way. You're thin, boy."
"Food doesn't nourish me. Men cannot live on bread only, not even brown bread made at home."
"No"
"Now in the moon, perhaps, I should get fat."
"Perhaps indeed, and I too. But look at the moon. You give me the horrors. You couldn't live there."
It was a thin three-quarters of a circle in a hot sky.
"But," I said, *" I should like to try."*
"Would you?"
"Yes, provided I were someone different. For, as for me, this is no doubt the best of all possible worlds."

"Better than the moon?"

"Yes, better than the moon; and there is nothing better in it than your well water, missus. Good afternoon."

The old map shows 'Shapens'. It seems the most likely location for this encounter, a small two-sided courtyard formed of two cottages and a range of barns and outbuildings that is long gone. There is now no visible evidence of this site, just a corner of an otherwise large arable field and a small copse following the line of the path. Rather eerily, within the copse, I encountered a post, a totem festooned with I know not what. The feathers of a selenite maybe.

Elsewhere along these miles of trackways is the site of the first colour illustration in Thomas book. *'Between Ickleton and Royston'.*

BETWEEN ICKLETON AND ROYSTON.

It appears to be sited several hundred yards after the tenth illustration, *'Approaching Royston'.* Both show an open landscape and a rutted trackway with low hills in the far distance. A building within a small cluster of trees in the middle distance appears similar in form but much closer in the painted illustration.

I took a photograph as close as I could get to what was called 'Kings Buildings' on the old map on the track's junction with Barley Road. The site is just visible in the photo, marked by a tree to the left of the overhead power line but the buildings themselves are now hidden by the hedgerow shrubs that have grown up on the line of the track. At the point from which I took the photo, the track was wide enough to take a four-wheeled cart but as it continued towards Barley Road it narrowed to a single wheel track. Then the verdure continued to close in until the thorns greeted each other across what little was left of the track as it approached the junction.

The site of the photo is closer to Barley Road than the illustration but much further away than the coloured illustration.

The distant hills have a more significant presence on the horizon in the coloured illustration than in the pencil sketch. In the photo they are all but invisible. I am unsure if this is the result of some artistic licence by Collins or, more likely, the result of using a modern, relatively wide-angle lens.

The track continued beyond Barley Road until it joined the A505 on the approach to Royston.

The Hertfordshire and Cambridgeshire border once chiselled its way around the perimeter of Royston following the line of the field boundaries. Now it takes a smoother line, following the route of the bypass that encompasses the extended built-up area. When Thomas passed this way, it was a small cluster of a town hugging Ermine Street, the north-south road that ran through it, structuring its form.

Royston

Thomas entered the town along Melbourn Street and continued along Baldock Street beyond the crossing point of the Icknield Way and Ermine Street. This crossing is the site of the eleventh illustration, *'Crossing Ermine Street'*.

This uncluttered street scene looks north along Ermine Street. The tall chimneys of King James Palace can be seen at the far end of the vista with the timber-framed buttery next door, jettying out over the pavement just behind the carter.

There has been quite a lot of demolition on the cross to open up the sightlines of the junction for modern traffic. It has created a not too convincing town square complete with a public toilet block. A leftover from a civic-minded age that ended somewhere between Thomas time and our own. I'd say, if pushed, 1979.

The illustration was sited in the High Street about fifty yards to the south of the cross. The jettying upper floor of what appears to have been a gas-lit cobblers' shop is still visible. The building with the projecting bay window at first-floor level opposite has gone. Old photos on the internet indicate that this was a cafeteria when Thomas passed by. The first building beyond the cross, behind the chap with the barrow, was the Crown Hotel, it was demolished in 1929. The other large building on the right-hand side of the junction has also been demolished and was the premises of Frost & Co. early in the twentieth century. The old map indicates a PH next to Frost & Co. Many of the pubs appear to be in the High Street which was off Thomas route through the town. Thomas mentions none of them.

It was market day when Thomas passed through, he could not decide whether to refer to Royston as a big village or a small town with its market, corn exchange, brewery, hotels, station and pubs. It has grown considerably since, consolidating its case to be regarded as a town.

Odsey

Beyond Royston, Thomas had but a couple of miles or so to travel to Odsey along the Cambridgeshire and Hertfordshire border. By Thrift Farm the old map shows a Horse and Groom about halfway to Odsey. It appears to have been derelict for many years. It is squeezed tight against the eastbound carriageway of the now duelled A505. As this road improvement has taken away at least half of its passing trade, its condition is no surprise.

Circumspect as ever about his overnight lodging, Thomas only revealed that it was a house he had never seen or heard described. As he approached, he drifted into one of his reveries:

"The air was silent and still, the road was empty. The birds coming home to the quiet earth seemed visitors from another world. They seemed to bring something out of the sky down to this world, and the house and garden where I stayed at last were full of this something."

Even today there is a large country house at Odsey, a Palladian Mansion built for the second Duke of Devonshire in 1723. There is a Grange too and no less suitable, the old map reveals a Travelers Rest pub next to the railway station.

The Travelers Rest, Odsey.

The Travelers Rest now trades under the name The Jester. Thomas narrative implies that he stayed at Odsey House. It would take a trawl through his archive to turn up a piece of correspondence that could clarify this matter. Such intensive research is well beyond the scope I have embraced in this account. Short of that proof, it is just as likely that he stayed here. Now in a lane off the A505 which also gives access to the Ashwell & Morden Railway Station, it would then have been a modest pub. Slate roof, flint faced walls with brick quoins to the corners and around the windows, all the hallmarks of a Victorian pub. The pub probably came with the railway and consequently has an urban rather than a rural aesthetic and is constructed from the mass-produced materials of the industrial age rather than from local ones. It has been much extended in recent years. Aspects of the style of place it was in Thomas time remain in the earlier parts of the building. Plain, low ceilings, a curved brick fireplace, plain timber wainscot with built-in settles around the walls and a plain timber fronted bar. Some of the features may well be later but the overall feel has probably not changed that much. The footprint of the building as extended is far greater, however. It is carpeted and undergoing redecoration as I sit here.

It is never possible to say whether any of the many punctuations to the normal narrative, like his encounter at Shapens, were not pure invention. Looking for some strangeness to relieve the orthodoxy of describing the botanical wonders on each side of the road. It is perhaps surprising that he made no mention of the Royston Cave, that supposed shrine of the Templar Order and perhaps precursor of Damanhur. Discovered in 1742 and dating probably from the thirteenth century, it is now an established visitor attraction. Perhaps less so in 1911. Among the many carvings on the cave walls are representations of St Christopher and St Catherine. St Cristopher is pertinent to Thomas many travels and St Catherine to the nearby Nuthampstead Zodiac.

Thomas would not have known that the zodiac was nearby, though he did suggest that the Way may have once passed through Barley to the south of Royston. A village nestled in Pisces, Thomas birth sign.

In my previous book, I noted the points at which Thomas route took him through parts of the Kingston and the Glastonbury Zodiacs. Thomas would have been unaware of this as neither had been proposed when he passed that way. The Glastonbury Zodiac was first proposed by Katherine Maltwood in 1929 in her book *"A Guide to Glastonbury's Temple of the Stars"*, the Kingston Zodiac, not until the 1970s with the publication of Mary Cain's book *"The Kingston Zodiac"*. Had he been aware of them, maybe he would have included a passing comment in his narrative. I was aware the Icknield Way passed by the edge of the Nuthampstead Zodiac but not through it. It is not something I had originally planned to make any reference to. Idly searching on the internet, not specifically on the trail of either Thomas or the Icknield Way at that time, I came across a reference to the Welsh Zodiac. A proposition that was quite new to me. This Zodiac was proposed by Lewis Edwards in 1944. What arrested my attention was that it was called the Pumpsaint Zodiac. It is a correspondence of sorts for Thomas wrote the dedication and maybe large sections of the Icknield Way at the Dolau Cothi Arms in Pumpsaint.

CHAPTER 3

THIRD DAY — ODSEY TO EDLESBOROUGH, BY BALDOKCK, LETCHWORTH, ICKLEFORD, LEAGRAVE AND DUNSTABLE

A brief description of the route:

On day three Thomas travelled about 30 miles. The dual carriageway that has replaced the road Thomas trod continues through Hertfordshire to just outside Baldock. Beyond Baldock, Thomas travelled on roads and trackways that had already begun to be subsumed it into Letchworth. What, on the old map even then had the look of an edgeland countryside has become the Luton and Dunstable massif. He captures the first meaningful site of the Downs in Dunstable marking a change in the landscape that would accompany him for the rest of his journey.

***

The following morning Thomas continued along a road now passing through a gently undulating countryside of vast, wide-open skies. Much of Thomas journey passed through a sparsely populated countryside. Towns like Royston and Newmarket and those he had yet to encounter occupied a mere fraction of the land they do now. In the case of Royston the 0.25 square miles it covered in 1911 has expanded nearly seven times over the past 100 years to 1.65 square miles and in the case of Newmarket, its 0.275 square miles has increased nine-fold to 2.5 square miles. We have yet to confront Luton. In 1911, 0.875 square miles and now taking in just the landmass to the east of the M1, excluding Dunstable and its hinterland to the west of the M1, now 15 square miles or a 17.5 times increase. While the open countryside has clearly changed in more nuanced ways it is hard to over exaggerate the scale of change to the towns he passed through.

Just beyond Odsey he left Cambridgeshire behind and would have passed the Hare and Hounds, now buried under a farmyard and bungalow. The Icknield Way continues to run parallel to what was then the Great Northern Railway as they both approached Baldock. The A505 dual carriageway at last peals away to the south just outside Baldock and from the intersection, the B656 continues the line of the Icknield Way towards the town past the Ashville Trading Estate and acres of late-twentieth-century housing.

Baldock

Thomas mentions the Toll Bar Inn which he passed on the edge of the town. It is long gone, as a pub at least. An old photo on the internet reveals it as a purveyor of 'Pages Ales' rather than 'Simpsons of Baldock' which then enjoyed a significant presence in the towns watering holes. Despite the extensive redevelopment in the area, the rump of the building itself has been incorporated into this later development. Its presence in this otherwise comprehensively redeveloped area, however, seems incongruous rather than contextual. The Way skirts around the town centre to the north along what Thomas regarded as a "...*sordid lane called Bygrave Lane or Deadman's Lane.*" He names three pubs, the Stag, the Swan and the Black Eagle. It is the site of the next illustration, No.12: *'Deadmans Lane, Baldock'*.

The three pubs were arranged along the left-hand side of the street. Modern housing has replaced all the buildings that Thomas would have based his judgement on. It appears to be a view from a little before the junction with Norton Street, Church Street as it is now, looking west. Apart from the shape of the re-engineered road, it is all but unrecognisable.

An old photo on the internet shows Bygrave Lane in the early twentieth century. It is taken from almost the same spot as the illustration. In it, the street is populated by its residents. They appear to be maintaining an air of pride and respectability in the kind of circumstances that befall people in this age as well as that one. Seen against this photograph, Thomas assessment seems rather harsh.

Thomas mentions the *"Sand Boys"* in passing. They traded sand which was then used as a sweep clean covering to the floors of pubs. An alternative to the more commonly referenced 'spit and sawdust'. Presumably, these Sandboys were 'happy' with three pubs in such close proximity. Thomas statement that they traded bone and rabbit skins for the sand suggests they were of Gypsy stock and in the same sentence claims that Bygrave Lane was the *"...reputed scene of the death of Gypsy Smith's wife and his own conversion."* Gypsy Rodney Smith was then a well known evangelist who joined what later became the Salvation Army. Later in life, he evangelised on his own account in Britain and overseas but it was his mother, not his wife that died. The family visited the town when one of his sisters fell ill, to seek the help of a doctor. Diagnosing smallpox, the doctor sent them from the town to camp in one of the nearby lanes. From here, their tale is a harrowing one but for Rodney:

"It was my mother's death, however, which woke me to full consciousness, if I may so put it. This event made a wound in my heart, which has never to this day been really healed"

It was this experience that set in train the events that led him, at the age of sixteen, to embark on his lifelong mission as an evangelist. There is no indication in the book that Thomas was an admirer of Gypsy Smiths poetry and judging by Thomas frequent judgements on the religious sentiments left by the living on the monuments to the dead, his opinion is probably best left unknown.

Following the route of the Icknield Way, Thomas would have seen little of the town centre with its broad, central, pub filled street and marketplace. Then, Baldock was a small discrete town in open countryside gathered around a crossroad. It now has its suburban extensions but in terms of scale at least has become the minor, overshadowed partner next to the much expanded Letchworth.

The route Thomas took beyond Norton Road can no longer be followed, housing, an industrial estate and the A1M have obliterated it and now a rather convoluted route across a new footbridge linking Coachman's Lane and the Letchworth Industrial Estate is required to eventually link up with the original alignment at Norton Common.

Letchworth Garden City

The Garden City was growing rapidly when Thomas passed this way and what had been an ancient track became, *"...a garden-city street called Icknield Way."*

As Thomas approached the town he was greeted *by:*

"...a building gigantically labelled 'IDRIS.' This was, I suppose, the temple of this city's god, though the name, except as the Welsh equivalent for Arthur, was unknown to me. They say now that Arthur was a solar hero, and when in doubt men might do worse than to worship the sun, if they could discover how. At Letchworth they were endeavouring to do so. The sun was not benign or even merciful in return for these efforts. He responded by telling the truth with his most brilliant beams, so that the city resembled a caravan of bathing machines, except that there was no sea and the machines could not conveniently be moved."

Cynical as ever about anything not of the old countryside, for once he showed at least an awareness of the more noble intentions of Letchworth in comparison with much that went before with the little aside,

"...Letchworth may turn out to be an exception."

And it was an exception, at that time at least. It is hard not to overemphasise the radical change in lifestyle that Letchworth aspired to because the depravations it sought to respond to are now beyond living memory. Despite this, the principles and aspirations it was founded on still speak to the present. It also seems remarkable that it took just five years from the publication of Ebenezer Howards book, *'Tomorrow: a Peaceful path to real reform'* in 1898 to the formation of the First Garden City Ltd in 1903.

A resident describing the early days of the City:

"They were great days! Garden City was very young and full of promise. A large proportion of the first immigrants – the pioneer settlers were young married folk, poor but bursting with hope and idealism. We were very sociable and there was a complete absence of class consciousness.... No doubt we were "cranks". Socialism, vegetarianism, simple life, bare legs and no hat, and so on, were innovations which provoked the derision of visiting journalists. These oddities were peculiar to us at the time but became common enough everywhere a few years later."

An open-hearted herald of an age of hope that expressed an energy that others have spent their own lifetimes attempting to expunge from modern consciousness. There being no alternative. The clock may turn, but not the derision of journalists, political fundamentalists and the elites that fund them.

Wilbury Hill Camp punctuates the point where the Icknield Way returns to open countryside on the western edge of Letchworth and is the location of the next illustration, No.13: *'Wilbury Camp'*.

A Bronze age fort, the camp is easy to find, sitting next to a pub of that name, or so I thought. It has been inundated with nettle and thorn thickets. Though I bravely fought my way through them, I struggled to find any topography as dramatic as that in the illustration. Checking the map again I realised I was floundering about in an old gravel pit. Eventually, I crossed to the other side of the Stotford Road and in a corner of land found the site of the illustration. It too is now swamped with an almost impenetrable barrier of verdure almost indistinguishable from the gravel pit. Not photographable now in any recognisable way.

Ickleford

Beyond Wilbury, the Way becomes a track again dividing the counties of Bedfordshire and Hertfordshire as it continues into Ickleford by way of a level crossing, now a footbridge; over the Great Northern Railway, the vanished Midland Railway and then through the ford over the River Oughton and to the site of the next illustration, No. 14: *'The ford Ickleford'*.

This pastoral scene is little changed but for two things, well three things. Pastoral agriculture has been all but expunged from this part of England, the ford has been bridged and the unmanaged growth of the verdure forms a visually impenetrable wall beyond the water's edge.

Beyond the ford the Way still enters the village of Ickleford next to Upper Green and the church, the site of the next Illustration, No.15: *Ickleford Church'*.

About the only change to St Katherines Church is the size of the cedar trees that dominate the churchyard even more than in Thomas time.

The Old map shows the Icknield Way continuing south west to the south of the church past the Old George and the Green Man, along Turnpike Lane. Thomas mentions both pubs, the Old George still trades but the Green Man is no more.

Ickleford has grown substantially to the north of the Icknield Way but perhaps more significantly, Hitchin and its attendant industrial estates has crept ever closer. Ickleford is now an almost barely separated suburb. However, when Thomas passed this way and despite it being a separate and more ancient settlement, Ickleford had caught some of the modernising Letchworth buzz.

The Old George, Ickleford.

A very picturesque timber-framed pub with a large inglenook and a stone floor. The timbers have been painted terracotta and a colour I could call puce, others might call mushroom. That is not to say that the overall effect is not attractive. A rustic sawn timber bar front and wainscot together with the timber topped tables and painted chairs complete the picture. The ubiquitous IPA and Abbot relieved by the glorious Summer Lightning that Thomas, also, might have been delighted to come across.

Ickleford seemed to be in tune with the new vibe at large in the early days of the garden city. As a contemporary local newspaper report stated.

"For Ickleford lies within the sphere of social experiment... though there may be no actual connection in the nature of cause and effect, it seems not very surprising that prophets of the social redemption should rise up in that country."

The Ickleford Industries of Applied Art flourished under the direction of Walter, Marian and Arthur Witter, providing training in skills and offering employment to the young in fine metalwork, leatherwork, needlecrafts, woodwork and ceramics against the background of the otherwise declining employment opportunities in rural communities at that time. The production and output had much in common with the Arts and Crafts Movement. There were exhibitions of the work each year which, it would seem, gained interest and commissions from across the country and even Europe. These days the countryside's young are not so cosseted and expected to move aside for second homeowners. Instead of exhibitions of their work, we see illustrations in any one of the many country homes magazines of how some simpering Samantha and Gerry have transformed one of these once humble dwellings into a fantasy rural weekend retreat.

~

Beyond Ickleford the way continues as a single carriageway road with passing places as far as West Mill where it reverts to a track again across some open, very subtly undulating countryside. It continues beyond the Hitchin Road till it shares its route briefly with the B655 Hexton Road. The folds in the land start to become more intense as the track peals away from the road along the edge of the Bedfordshire border heading towards Telegraph Hill and the site of the next illustration, No. 16: *'On Telegraph Hill'*.

The illustration is a view back along the track as it passes through a deep embankment. Trees and undergrowth have colonised this area and the track now follows around the top of the embankment rather than through it. The older path is now blocked by a thicket at its western end, in fact, I was not able to penetrate it further than the location from which I took the photo and consequently could not gain access to the exact site of the original illustration.

Thomas was 650 feet above sea level at this point:

"It is difficult to understand why it should make this climb instead of circumventing the hill by a sharp curve southward. It never again does such a thing or rises to such an altitude."

From here the track descends two hundred feet to where it briefly joins the Hexton Road just before entering Bedfordshire then reverting to a track past Galley Hill and what is now the South Beds Golf Course and then Drays Ditch on Luton's edgelands. Dray Ditch, the fourth and last of the series of Saxon defensive ditches, marks what is now the start of Luton. Luton was still nearly 3 miles away when Thomas passed this way. The post-war housing developments of cul-de-sacs confound the route Thomas followed to the sixteenth milestone on what is now the A6.

Luton

Even then Luton was on the move, development was already spreading out from the outlying villages before merging into the greater Luton and Dunstable conurbation. There follow several miles of urban-suburban dual carriageway that was then countryside. Bungalows to the right, a mown verge to the left then bungalows all the way to the roundabout at Limbury. Well, mostly bungalows. There is now a Jolly Milliner pub on this route. Thomas crossed the marsh to Leagrave and the Three Horseshoes pub. He presumed that Leagrave Marsh had once been a *"pleasant little ford village"* but was still able to describe the scene before him thus:

"At one side of the bridge the 'Three Horse Shoes' faced over the common and along the water; ponies, traps, and dogs were clustered at the door in the sun. Their owners were either inside, getting hot, or lying on the grass over the way. But one driver was taking his horse and trap through the stream close to the bridge; and the whipped foam was shining and the spokes flashing. Some boys were paddling a little way above; and above them the village geese were nibbling among the rush tufts. In and out among horses and traps, men, dogs, boys, and geese, the martins were flying."

Difficult to visualise now, the Three Horse Shoes has been replaced by a McDonalds on a busy gyratory complete with a petrol station, pelican crossings and congestion. The River Lea passes under this urban hotspot almost unseen.

Thomas continued south-west under what was then the Midland Railway and into Leagrave. Here he would have passed the Sugar Loaf pub and entered:

"...the brand-new, jerry-built, slated cages of combined Limbury"

Thomas appears to have turned left at what he called Oak Road, perhaps now Oakley Road, past the long closed Royal Oak pub and through a field he described as *"rotten-ripe"* for building.

"This road interrupted my way, which went formerly as a footpath straight across it and into the main road a little west of the Half-way House, between Dunstable and Luton. This path was ploughed up and its course only in part noticeable among the crops."

This footpath followed the line of what is now Stoneygate Road. It turns to the south as it joins the A505 Dunstable and Luton Road to the east of the Halfway House pub. The pub is now the site of a Travelodge. Here the M1 crashes over the environs of Leagrave.

The gyratory under the M1 is an unpleasant traverse for a pedestrian, the once tranquil track unimaginable. From here the Way continues as the A505 dual, urban highway and crosses the railway, now a busway, and on into Dunstable. Yes, I traversed Luton's suburbs at speed and I'm sure it shows.

Dunstable

"As I entered Dunstable there was already a touch of night in the light, and it fell with a sad blessing upon the low-towered church and the sheep grazing in the churchyard..."

Dunstable is now more or less contiguous with Luton rather than the self-contained town it was in 1911. Now, only the M1 separates them. The old map indicates four pubs along Church Street as it approaches the town centre, though there were more. Among them the First and Last, Norman King, Red Lion, Royal Oak and White Horse. All gone. The town was originally defined by the intersection of the Icknield Way and Watling Street crossing and now sits in the centre of a myriad of new crossing points of much less significance. The crossing is the site of the next illustration, No. 17: *'Icknield Way crossing Watling Street Dunstable'*. It is just to the east of the cross on the left of Church Street looking west along West Street.

Similar in form to the crossing in Royston, this A5 Watling Street junction looked tight and classically urban in the illustration, the corners dominated by pubs, hotels and banks. Like Royston, subsequent demolition has opened up the sightlines for modern traffic resulting in a much more diffuse, low grade, cluttered modern street scene.

Continuing along West Street, Thomas would have passed the Rifle Volunteer where West Street becomes Tring Road. A wayside pub giving way to residential expansion and street widening, it is now under the junction of the B489 and B4541. The edge of the built-up area now extends nearly a mile beyond the point it finished in 1911. Thomas was able to comment on the views of the downs long before they now come into view. From Dunstable on, the Downs become ever present to the left, retreating and advancing towards the Icknield Way in turns, sometimes a smudge on the horizon sometimes dominating the road.

As the road swept around to the south beyond the Rifle Volunteer, Thomas passed a series of chalk pits. Chalk extraction is still an important industry in Dunstable and the modern Kensworth Quarry large enough to swallow virtually the whole of Dunstable as it was in 1911.

As Thomas left Dunstable along the B489, evening was drawing closer. He remarks on the proximity of the Downs, which he also calls the Chilterns by turns, to the east of his road. Today, only glimpses of the downs can be caught between the buildings on the route out of Dunstable. Somewhere beyond here is the site of the next illustration, No. 18: *'Dunstable Downs'*.

The illustration has all the hallmarks of an image taken from a photograph, yet I struggle to identify the exact location. The illustration shows what is at least a three-way and maybe a four-way guidepost with one finger pointing towards the 'camera'. So, this is either on a crossroad or tee junction. The curving track beyond the guidepost suggests that it may be a crossroad with the fourth finger of the guidepost hidden from this angle. The old map shows the first crossroad, beyond the town's edge, to be next to the Rifle Volunteer pub. The old map also indicates that this junction had a guidepost but the road heading south, next to the pub is straight, not curved like the one in the illustration. However, this area is now so built up that the views of the downs are almost completely obscured. The next guidepost shown on the old map is two or three miles beyond Dunstable where the Plough Inn once sat on what is now the B4506.

The pub became the New York Dinner for a while but is now closed. There is a roundabout on this junction now but even taking that into account the road geometry does not match the illustration. The next four-way junction is at the Travellers Rest pub but according to the old map, the guidepost is on the wrong side of the junction. Despite the introduction of a double roundabout here, again, the road geometry is all wrong. The site of some of the illustrations sometimes prove difficult to track down in the modern age. This is a case in point. It is easy to assume some artistic licence has been introduced and distorted what otherwise appears to be an accurate tracing of a photograph. The extensive tree and undergrowth that lines so many roads today often dramatically changes, if not completely obscures the modern view adding to the difficulty. The image seems to show a coombe to the left centre of the image and a cleft in the face of the downs to the right. I backtrack to Well Head, a 'T' junction rather than a crossroad. The old map does not show a guidepost here. It is on the junction of the B489 and Well Head Road, a C Class road heading north towards Totternhoe. There is now a track, the fourth arm of a crossroad leading to the London Gliding Club but this postdates 1911. What is not shown on the old map is a bridleway curving away from the road to the left. Before the hard surfacing of roads and when horse-powered transport was still commonplace, bridleways would have appeared as a part of the general road and track infrastructure just as this track appears in the illustration. Now it is quite separate, starting beyond the firm kerb line of the modern road. Trees completely block the view of the downs at this point now but following the bridleway into the field beyond, the view opens up. From this position and as it is much lower down, it cannot be an exact match but the now wooded cleft can be seen in the face of the downs and the coombe, now also wooded, curves from right to left in the foreground.

So is this the location of the illustration or as close as I can get to it in the modern world. It ticks several boxes but I've not convinced myself. Something in the shape of the downs at this point seems amiss. I return to the Travellers Rest. The verdure here now obscures the downs but from a location several hundred yards from the pub, where there is a break in the treeline, the crest of the downs, with that nearly horizontal line with the shallow dip to the left, matches the illustration. The old map shows a line of springs and a stream in a coombe like feature in the middle distance and Dell Farm beyond where the group of buildings at the foot of the downs in the illustration appear. Returning to the Travellers Rest I cross what is now the A4146 where the ground rises along the Tring Road from where a partial view of the downs can be glimpsed.

From this orientation, the road in the foreground is the A4146 with the Icknield Way appearing as the small adjoining road curving away to the left. The now tree capped downs look about right, the line of the coombe is marked by the line of mature trees in the middle distance, the Travellers Rest is on the far left. It also ticks many of the boxes but the guidepost is in the wrong place. I'm not sure I can separate these choices.

On the approach to the Travellers Rest, Thomas had crossed the border into Buckinghamshire as dusk began to settle.

"...the sky was light and its clouds of utmost whiteness were very wildly and even fiercely shaped, so that it seemed the playground of powerful and wanton spirits knowing nothing of earth."

Continuing, he slipped gently into one of his end of day reveries.

As *"The air was now still and the earth growing dark and already very quiet."* he fell in with what he refers to as a philosopher who was pondering a dichotomy in his sense of self. It was 'an other' man but of an altogether more introspective and poetic disposition to the Other Man that shared Thomas Pursuit of Spring and more definitely, Thomas himself. *"half his life lay behind him like a corpse, so he said, and half was before him like a ghost"*. He was unable to divine whether he felt *"happiness or melancholy"* at the end of a gruelling day. As he absorbed and described the morphing landscape before him as the sunset *"Slowly the solid world was whittled away"*, then *"The quiet, the magnitude of space, the noble lines of the range a little strengthened his spirit"*. Reflecting on his place in the world *"Of young men he was now sometimes jealous; of middle-aged men afraid and no longer defiant. Towards the contemporaries with whom he had shared thought and experience for some years he felt jealousy, if he seemed to have outstripped them in the unwilling race; fear, if it was himself that lagged; and towards only one or two a fair and easy freedom, and that only intermittently"*. A peel of music rang out in the darkness breaking the bond of introspection as a *"liquid voice mounted in its beautiful, unseen form amidst the darkness... It was a powerful voice, confident and without care. It leapt up with a wild, indolent flight, for one short verse of indistinguishable words"* in the distance. When the sound ended, he imagined the songstress in the quiet company of her lover and mourned his own isolation *"...and he went into his house and it was dark and still and inconceivably empty."*

Turning away, breaking the spell, Thomas entered the Travelers Rest and encountered a complete change of atmosphere as he was engaged by a *"...jaunty, probably childless London woman not far from forty"* with *"...a skittish, falsetto laugh"*.

Travelers Rest

[London Pride, Bombardier, Doombar]

This is a much upscaled pub. The original part of the building, the part Thomas would have visited has a modern homely feel, low ceilings with the timbers exposed, a rustic open fireplace, a timber boarded floor and neat timber panelling lining the walls, neither of which look original. The furniture, a mixture of leather chesterfield sofas, armchairs and settles. The windows are curtained, and ornate table lamps give a finishing touch to a look that Thomas would struggle to recognise as the interior of a pub. It is also a long way from the house the Londoners would have kept. For a pub of the modern age, it has been thoroughly and successfully done. The completeness of the ambience that has been self-consciously created here leaves nothing to chance. It is an unambiguous statement of the modern commercialism that has visited many of the more successful pubs and pub chains in recent years. It provides a customer experience and a reliable, measurable, predetermined level of service. Maybe there were pubs with this kind of aspiration in Thomas time though that seems unlikely. One thing such pubs are not, is a focus of community life, more a place of anonymity. There is no traction with Thomas reverie in this kind of environment, it satiates the senses with its own self-conscious narrative.

We can become distracted from ourselves in such a place.

However, Thomas encounter with the philosopher is one of the more poetic episodes in his book that pays reading in full. It reveals Thomas almost pagan reverence for the human experience of the countryside as it quietly reveals the spiritual magic of the transformation from day to night when his sense of isolation was at its most acute. There is a confessional judgement against his relationship with his peers, self-worth and a nagging dissatisfaction with his accomplishments. The almost intangible discrimination between happiness and melancholy, identifying but not quite articulating the law of opposites. He was clearly capable of pondering such matters.

It is, in one sense, an abstract celebration in the gathering darkness of the human power to add imagination to the sensory inputs of existential experience.

~

CHAPTER 4

FOURTH DAY — EDLESBOROUGH TO STREATLEY, ON UPPER ICKNIELD WAY BY WENDOVER, KIMBLE, WHITELEAF, GIPSIES CORNER, IPSDEN AND CLEEVE

A brief description of the route:

At about 40 miles, this was the longest section of Thomas journey. The character of the walk begins to change as Thomas heads up into the hills. To begin with, he catches a lift, travelling on conventional roads and following the Upper Icknield Way from the dividing point near Ivinghoe as far as Butlers Cross. From here he walks on a mixture of what, even now, is a mixture of conventional C Class roads, trackways and footpaths, then a consistent section of defined footpath follows, along the edge of the Chilterns before returning to a mixture of C Class roads and paths for the last section of this journey into Goring on Thames.

***

Thomas was woken the following morning at five by the landlady's husband, a:

"*...little active man, superficially jaunty but silent and brooding and* *hanging down his head. He was sandy-haired with dull, restless, blue eyes, and had not recently been shaved."*

For someone who seemed to regularly walk parts of the Pilgrims Way perhaps these Chaucerian vignettes are appropriate. Thomas uses them effectively throughout the narrative.

Thomas had the longest leg of his journey in front of him, some forty miles. He was footsore and therefore grateful for the lift in the horse and trap that was on offer to him. He set off with Mr Willocks along the B489. After less than a mile they were winding around the edge of Beacon Hill, the site of next illustration, No. 19: *'Beacon Hill Ivinghoe'*.

This illustration is taken beyond the Beacon on the B489 looking back. It is just before the junction with the B488. The rampant hedgerow has stripped the landscape, as represented in the illustration, of its rawness and majesty. At best, now a piecemeal view of the two hillsides softened and reduced by the creeping encapsulation of modern tree cover. Road signs, kerb lines and pothole repairs do little to enhance the view. Even the overhead lines detract but then again, where they add character to Collins illustrations elsewhere, this is probably more the result of the artist hand than real life.

Beyond Beacon Hill, on this junction just before Ivinghoe, the way divides into the Lower Icknield Way and the Upper Icknield Way. Here, a footpath also leads to the Pitstone Windmill. Thomas speculated that this might be an older section of the Way from a time when the two routes forked rather than divided at an engineered 'T' junction as now. Thomas continued along the Upper Icknield Way. A mile or so beyond the junction, the Way was briefly joined by the Buckinghamshire and Hertfordshire border. After crossing over what was the London and North Western Railway, they reached the Grand Junction Canal and re-entered Hertfordshire and the site of the next illustration.

Bulbourne

Illustration No. 20: *'Grand Junction Canal'*, appears to have been taken from the bridge over the canal looking south-east. The left bank is now completely colonised by a dense tree cover and the view of the open countryside, obscured beyond the first curve in the canal. The Edwardian telegraph posts have gone. According to the old map, the buildings in the middle distance would have been Parkhill Farm. The Grand Junction Arms sits practically on the bridge.

G rand Junction Arms, Bulbourne.

[IPA and Tring Brewery's Side Pocket]

Thomas did not mention the pub. An old, rather plain pub whose principal merit today is the large canal-side beer garden. Clearly an attraction to families with young children. Inside is a clay tiled floor, painted wainscot and a timber fronted bar shaped to suggest something nautical. In contrast to the Travellers Rest and apart from the modern food offer, this place is not that different from the type of simple roadside pub that Thomas might have been familiar with early in the last century. Its character suggests it was originally intended for canal workers. The Travellers Rest is completely overlaid by the modern world, only a subjective form of archaeology can strip that back to the pub Thomas knew. The Grand Junction Arms is much more lightly touched by the modern world but even this is enough to leave only fuzzy hints at the appearance of Thomas world and nothing of its dynamic.

Freestanding pubs, like the Grand Junction Arms seem able to adapt to change across generations with only relatively minor structural alterations. This is not always the case with other building types. Old photos of Victorian and Edwardian street scenes often display a sense of visual cohesiveness and to mangle a term to adequately describe it, 'groundedness'. The buildings seem rooted to the land they stand on. In the modern era, the character of many shopping streets has changed dramatically since then. This goes beyond old buildings being replaced by new ones and we get a hint of it in Pursuit where Thomas expresses his disdain for plate glass. That relatively new technology was already beginning to transform commercial street frontages. The ground floors of shops are often stripped away without regard to the upper floors to insert new frontages at ground level that conform to modern retail orthodoxy. The outcome is to divest these buildings from their original 'groundedness' and is a contributory cause of the loss of the visual continuity that once existed in our more historic town centres. One of the consequences of this loss is that the upper floors of these buildings are often demoted to secondary uses as the commercial and social dynamic changed. In more extreme cases, they have fallen increasingly into dereliction as their social function was drained away, as residential use moved out into the suburbs. While modern town centres can stand alone, it is in older provincial towns and secondary shopping streets where this uncomfortable clash of the past and present is most often evident.

The illustrations numbered 11, *'Crossing Ermine Street'* and 17, *'Icknield Way crossing Watling Street Dunstable'* graphically display how the tight urban core of what were once small towns has been eroded, where cohesiveness and 'groundedness' has been lost and leaves in its place an incoherent environment that can no longer sustain any desire to linger.

~

A little further on, towards Tring, was the Queens Arms, lost under a roundabout and new housing. Tring was then a modest town, still in the middle distance. The substantial suburbs of Tring were still a mile away in 1911 but have now expanded up to the edge of the Way itself.

On the line of what was the junction with Akeman Street, the Way now flies over the duelled A41. It connects with the old Akeman Street, now the B4009, on the other side. Thomas followed this road along Tring Hill for about a mile to the next left-hand turn and the continuation of the Upper

Icknield Way towards Wendover. Thomas typically remarked that

"This space beside Tring Hill should have been a common for ever; but either it never was or a common award handed it over to the largest mouth."

Perhaps more in Pursuit than in this book, Thomas makes it perfectly clear that he believed that such land should have always remained in the hands of true country folk whose interests were so often trumped by the avaricious, entitled and connected. Some things show few signs of change.

Thomas passed through the woodlands of what he considered the *"polite"* Halton House. It is now the Officers Mess of RAF Halton. Had he passed this way today he might well have commented on the comparison between the officers' accommodation and the 'industrial unit' in which the sergeants' mess is housed.

Wendover

Thomas described Wendover as a *"long little town of cottages"*. According to the old map, in 1911 on Thomas route through the town it would have offered the Rose and Crown, the Pack Horse, the George Inn, the Red Lion, two more unnamed pubs in quick succession and another unnamed pub next to the railway.

The Pack Horse still trades next to row of thatched half-timbered cottages along with the George and Dragon in Aylesbury Road, the impressive Red Lion coaching inn and the Shoulder of Mutton next to railway. The Pack Horse was the subject of the next illustration; No. 21: *'Wendover'*.

While little seems changed in the form of the terrace of thatched cottages, everything seems changed. One can count the parked cars, contrast the blacktop road engineering with the surfaces of the trackways, single out the TV aerials maybe, the tended front gardens and the extravagant topiary, the pylons striding across the once wilder landscape, the trees covering the hillside and consuming the church tower but there is another, less tangible but nonetheless unmistakable, unreconcilable difference between the two images.

The illustration seems to capture a life moving at a different pace. One in which ordinary folk, maybe, had more limited horizons but a more grounded presence within its confines. It is impossible to remake Thomas world and the contrast between these two images suggests that it is impossible to even to understand it fully.

P ack Horse, Wendover.

[London Pride, Proper Job, and Gales Seafarers Ale]

I entered the pub looking out for a cottage wife with her dog, cat or is it a sheep and a couple of chickens and found a basic boozer. A plain, simple, single bar festooned with an extensive collection of brass, a large area given over to the dartboard and attendant trophy cabinet. A stove in an old brick fireplace, the timber mantle decorated with Victorian ceramic tiles.

A pub like this has probably been consistently serving the same type of clientele since at least Thomas time. Nothing is upscaled here, just unselfconsciously authentic. Such character cannot be extended to the town itself. That is not to single Wendover out for this, as it is true of many places. Authenticity, that firm connection between the past and the present is a characteristic that has declined rapidly since Thomas time. The later suburban development of Wendover has no affinity with the life that founded the town Thomas passed through. The acres of semidetached houses with their cul-de-sacs and carefully rationed gardens belong to a life unrecognisable. The residential streets given Drives, Closes, Crescents, Ways, Mews and Avenues without trees. It all seems so contrived, fake even.

~

Thomas crossed over what was the Metropolitan Railway just to the south of Wendover Station as he left the town. The Way crosses many railway lines, main lines as well as branch lines. A proportion were culled by Beeching. The character of most, probably had more in common with Edith Nesbit's 'The Railway Children' than Turner's 'Rain Steam and Speed' but that may be about to change. HS2 is planned to whisk past the edge of Wendover just yards to the east of the existing railway line, albeit in a tunnel. It will not be stopping.

Climbing the hill beyond, a panorama opens up to the right across the Aylesbury plain. Thomas would have passed the Russell Arms at Butlers Cross. He did not mention it though it still trades.

Ellensborough

Then on the approach to Ellensborough:

"The road went up and down, coming thus suddenly in sight of Ellesborough Church tower rising pale ahead out of its trees against the clear line of the hills."

Not anymore. Illustration No. 22: *'Ellensborough Church'* is taken beyond the church looking back uphill. Nothing can be seen of the church from this location now or the nearby house or the small barn shown in the foreground of the illustration. All obscured by modern verdure.

The small barn in the foreground is still at the foot of the hill, almost unchanged.

Great Kimble

At Great Kimble Thomas got down from the cart to resume his walk outside the Bear and Cross. It would be a fair assumption that he took refreshment here, maybe buying one for Mr Willcock by way of thanks.

The pub was renamed the Bernard Arms at some point, perhaps when the large extension that dominates the original building was added. It appears to have been closed for some years. It is now completely derelict, so I am unable to sample its virtues.

About half a mile beyond Great Kimble Thomas took a track off to the right that led up to Whiteleaf and the Red Lion, a pub that still trades. This area was the subject of a number of artworks by both Paul Nash and his brother John. Thomas got to know Paul Nash when they were both stationed near Gidea Park in Essex in the war years and was known to have spent some of their off duty hours walking in an Essex countryside to which Thomas became attached.

The Red Lion, Whiteleaf.

[Chiltern Session IPA, Harvest Ale and Hawaiian Shirt]

It keeps the sense of a wayside pub, a rustic feel, some parts little changed since Thomas passed this way. Quaint, diminutive inside with a timber floor, settles, loose dark wood furniture, nothing overstated. A place to relax into, a place to spend time in. If only that were possible.

The one piece of up to date technology is perplexing everybody. The landlord, sitting on the customers' side of the bar, engaging, chatting to locals admits that he does not know how the till works. The female bar worker struggles to input the sequence of information required to log a tab for one of the customers ordering food. The rituals embedded into the software of this computerised system far too clever for any of us. A series of simple instructions I am sure but does anybody really want to wade through that curse of the modern age, the operating manual.

In Thomas time a working knowledge of arithmetic would have been adequate but these once useful skills have been replaced by another less transparent orthodoxy. I hand the distracted barmaid a fiver and wait several minutes for my change as she is befuddled by the demands of a technology that has moved beyond a simple cash drawer. The landlord apologises. Hope and expectation confounded. He is old but the bar tender's youth even, has no catalysing power on this occasion. Frustration is distilled out of this confrontation between the human and digital worlds.

~

As if in sympathy, the next illustration, No.23: *'Whiteleaf Cross'* is now just a virtual representation of something that has passed beyond the human visual range.

From the road and facing hillside, it is now completely obscured by trees.

The illustration appears to have been taken higher up the hillside looking down on the road from where it gains a clear view of the cross and chalk embankment. This once dramatic view of the cross now offers nothing further than the next tree trunk or maybe the one after that. We have lost so many views of the countryside over the past hundred years. I have nothing against trees, clearly, we need to be planting many more. But we also need the protect and maintain other aspects of the public realm and through that, our connection with the countryside. We seem to have lost all sight of this through neglect, disinterest and making a virtue of austerity.

From the roadside, looking towards the cross, it is lost in the woodland.

Beyond Whiteleaf, the track now skirts around the edge of Princes Risborough which was still at least a mile away when Thomas passed this way. At the junction with the A4010, the track is diverted to the left along this road before re-establishing itself on the right about half a mile further on. Thomas crossed over one railway line then under another. The Way continues on a blacktop road as far as the junction with the Bedlow Ridge Road where it becomes a bridleway as it heads up towards Wain Hill. The foot of the climb is the only location I could find that looks anything like the site of the coloured illustration entitled *'Under the Chilterns [near the Leather Bottle]'*.

There is no adjacent high ground here, though the illustrations sightline appears to be about twenty feet above the neat hedgerow that lined the track. Even the surrounding trees seem to offer no suitable vantage point.

UNDER THE CHILTERNS [NEAR THE "LEATHER BOTTLE."]

My photo is taken at ground level, from here the prospect is far from commanding. Only the kink in the road betrays the location. This is not the only illustration that appears to be taken from a vantage point well above ground level. I wonder how this has been achieved. At ground level, the views are obscured by modern unmaintained hedgerow. The usefulness of a drone comes to mind.

Collins artistic skill has picked out the neatly clipped hedgerows lining the road, the trees in the middle distance providing definition and depth to his image, the hills beyond, a promise of a destination. By contrast, the modern view is ragged and unstructured, offering little to entice the walker to explore further.

The track climbs the hill through established woodland. The ground rises steeply to the left and plunges at a precipitous angle to the right. Glimpses of the Vale of Aylesbury appear through the trees at intervals. As it reached the Leather Bottle, the Way was now at its highest point since Telegraph Hill, about 600 feet. During this accent, the quietness of the woodland momentarily becomes present, only birdsong seeps through the stillness from a distant perch. I pause to listen, breathing it in, feeling the gentleness of the air movement, filtered through the trees with the sunlight. Then the sound of a jet scores a path through the sky. A reminder that the lifestream of the natural world goes on even though we do not always hear it and only occasionally witness it. Nature exists in its own right, regardless of our presence. Perhaps more now than in 1911 the awareness of our senses has grown beyond the classic five outward and five inward one's because such moments are even more distant from everyday life and thereby, more noteworthy and need that extra layer of interpretation to reconcile the feeling with the experience.

The Leather Bottle – if only

The Leather Bottle is sadly long gone, it closed in 1925. The approach is unexpected. Along a narrow track, past a series of maze like hedges then in one turn the hedge ends and there it is. It enjoyed such a remarkable off road location for a pub. Virtually unknown in this age. Coming across a wayside inn in a location like this now would be magical but improbable.

We miss something if the senses are defined by the classical Aristotelian senses alone. Given the chance, our interaction with the natural world can be much broader, can be much deeper than that facilitated through the filter of those senses alone. Memory, knowing, intuition, even some communion with other animals and organisms can be included.

Tentatively, some scientific disciplines are beginning to provide evidence that life is much more interconnected than our modern consciousness has been trained to acknowledge. Our inner ranting obscures it much of the time. Such a useful weakness to those whose interests are best served by keeping us distracted. There are moments of insight and clarity when we notice the environment around us and our connection with it. Birdsong was one of the things that Thomas was animated by, when he seemed to come closest to this kind of extra sensory connection. So much of the time in this book he makes no connection, but then there are those occasional moments of engagement on another level, most obviously in moments like his reverie in Odsey and outside the Travellers Rest in Edlesborough.

~

The site of the next illustration, No. 24: *'Near the Leather Bottle'* is just beyond, looking back towards the pub.

One of the chimneys can be discerned in the centre of the illustration peeking above the rising ground on the right.

Old photos on the internet show the Leather Bottle to have been a double fronted building with a central doorway bookended by timber-clad outbuildings. Then, it sat in the open with views over the Vale of Aylesbury rather than out of sight, submerged in this modern tree belt. The outbuildings have gone, substantial domestic extensions have replaced them but the central range, the old double-fronted pub remains. A garden with neatly clipped topiary just about asserts some defensible space in front of the former pub's entrance.

Looking back on the building now, it is hard to pick the building out from the screen of verdure. In fact, the original parts that were visible in Collins illustration are now hidden behind one of the later extensions. The rutted way is no more, just a neat narrow path obediently following the lines of the new boundary fence and hedge.

"The road was now narrower, confined by a hedge and bank on the right and the steep wall of the thorn and juniper on the left. Presently another deep track came slantwise down from Chinnor Hill towards Bledlow and crossed my way. Beyond this the vale was lovely..."

Surprisingly little has changed despite the growth of Chinnor. Though we are in one of those places where one can sense a less changed England, nothing lasts indefinitely. Beyond the Chinnor Road is the site of a modern, though disused, chalk quarry on another scale again to the many chalk pits that Thomas passed along the route and a sore on the landscape that nature is beginning to reclaim. Beyond the quarry, the Way shares its direction with the Watlington Branch Line Railway. It was disused for many years but is slowly being reclaimed by the modern age of nostalgia in the form of the Chinnor and Princes Risborough Railway. As these ways separate again near what was Aston Rowant Station, the A40 crosses the Way. A warning from an earlier age, for just a little further on the M40 now strikes its own line across the Way next to Beacon Hill. It is close to the location of the next illustration, No. 25: *'Near Watlington'*. It is sited beyond Beacon Hill looking north close to the spot where the M40 carves its way through the landscape. The deep gorge through the Chilterns, just out of sight at this point.

The photo is taken closer to the hill than the illustration as it loses definition amongst the modern hedgerow and wooded land from further away.

The generosity of the width of the tracks beyond, create their own unique character. It is mesmerising and transporting traversing this high, pedestrian landscape alone, the sightlines converging on an imaginary vanishing point where the track and horizon meet. Carried on an embankment topping the downs it overlooks the wide expanse of the flatlands to the west and another even more distant horizon. Closer still to Thomas experience in this confined stretch of little changed countryside.

Despite these benefits, from here Thomas seems to pass through the countryside as far as Goring at speed, passing little comment other than a rapid and brief description of the countryside he was passing through. This had been a particularly long leg. He had already declared that he was footsore at the start of the day. It suggests he had had just about enough at this point and could not wait to get to his destination in Goring. This entire leg, since Great Kimble, had been open countryside and before that, just Wendover. Little to relieve the monotony except to comment on the width of the track, its surface construction, the nearby flora. Miles, with just one pub to break the monotony. It seems that it had worn him down and in this mood, had offered up little new for him to comment on. A discouraging state of affairs when he was seeking material to fill a book. It is as though he resorted to transcribing his notes directly onto the page without embellishment.

Despite Thomas rather perfunctory narrative at this point, the illustrations keep on coming. The next, No. 26: *'Ewleme Cow Common'.*

It is just a couple of miles or so further along the track near Britwell Salome. The illustration looks back across the vale to the northeast towards Cookley Green over a still recognisable and classically bucolic English landscape, albeit one rendered photographically without the benefit of Collins artistic touch.

The modern landscape seems flatter, less well defined by comparison, to say nothing of the modern hedgerow.

Then within a few hundred yards is the next illustration; No. 27: the *'Sinodun Hills'*, this time swivelling through a hundred and eighty degrees, looking south-west across the Aylesbury Plain.

The chimney of Didcot Power Station becomes an evident feature of the landscape before the Sinodun Hills can be recognised by a traveller unfamiliar with this area, or well, by me at least. The chimney, moving in parallax against the hills as the track is followed towards the west. Slowly its impact diminishes, little by little.

Had I travelled this way just weeks earlier the chimney would have been joined by three cooling towers. Had I travelled this way one hundred years after Thomas journey, there would have been six.

The Sinodun Hill is also the location of the 'Wittenham Clumps', another of Paul Nash's subjects, this one he returned to again and again: *"The pyramids of my small world"*. Nash rendered his interpretation of the natural world through distinctly mystical and symbolic imagery often juxtaposing inanimate cultural objects of the modern age with the ancient. Before the demolition of the cooling towers, the outlook from the Ridgeway across the Aylesbury Plain with this real life juxtaposition of Didcot against the Wittenham Clumps must have seemed like one of Paul Nash's images made manifest. I'm sorry to have missed it. Thomas probably enjoyed conversations on the subject of their different approaches to the natural world as he walked with Nash in Essex but there seems little room for such things in his own narrative descriptions of the landscape in this book. Thomas is missing from so much of it. It is what makes this work so inaccessible. So often he just lists the plants, the birds, the landscape without identity, as an indexer. He approaches the environment like the map reader he was to become.

A little beyond Cow Common the Upper and Lower Icknield Ways meet and share the same track for about two hundred yards along Clacks Lane just south of the Old London Road. Looking at this meeting of the ways on the map, to me it seems just as likely that the Upper Way continued to Wallingford, the Lower Way to Goring. However.

Continuing south beyond Oakley Wood Thomas traversed Grim's Ditch. Part of a twenty-mile network of defensive ditches, this one, unlike the East Anglian dykes thought to be Iron Age in origin.

A little beyond the ditch, where the road meets Coxs Lane, the Way heads across country on an unmetalled track and the site of the next illustration, No. 28: *'Near Ipsden Oxon'*. This is a view looking back towards the north and Coblers Hill, close to where the Way crosses Church Lane.

If you look closely at the illustration and the modern photo, it is as if a hundred years ago, the path in the foreground kinked around a cluster of elders that it knew would be growing there in years to come.

A little further on is the site of the next illustration, No. 29: *'Near Cleave'*.

The title of this illustration proved to be misleading. I had assumed that it was close to Cleve, probably a view of Grove Farm. I spent some time exploring this area trying to find a view of the modern farm that matched the illustration in any way. According to the old map, some buildings remain in the modern farmyard but many have gone, others have been added. This did not explain the disjuncture. The road leading to Grove Farm runs downhill, that in the illustrations looks level. It transpired that the site of the illustration was in fact not that near Cleve after all but about a mile further back.

It is a view looking south-west towards Icknield Farm from Glebe Farm. Much, if not all of Icknield Farm has been demolished along with the hayricks and other features from the lost world that the illustration suggests. The adjacent land has been developed as a rather rustic business centre complete with a Skydiving and Airsports Centre. Virtually nothing is recognisable in the modern view except the curve of the road and the adjacent landform.

The road continues through Cleeve, a developing suburb at that time and on to Goring.

Goring and Streatley

Thomas would have crossed over the railway into Goring High Street possibly turning south along Red Cross Road then west again along Station Lane and Ferry Lane towards the site of the Roman ford. Here, he speculated that the Way originally crossed the river at this point where:

Ferry Lane goes straight up to the Reading road a quarter mile south of the Bull."

Satisfied with that, Thomas headed north along Manor Road to Goring's Church, St. Thomas a Becket. Here, it is as if the dam of the mind-numbing traverse across the open countryside of the past forty miles has burst and the flood gates open. We are treated to several diatribes in quick succession, Thomas relieved to at last to come across some material he could identify with. But first, an echo of his melancholy informs an episode of literary criticism inspired by the inscriptions he read on the tombstones in the churchyard:

*"John Lammas and of James, Ann, and Ruth Thresher on tombstones.
What clear visages of men and women these call up, each perfect in its
way, shorn of the uncertain, vague, or incongruous elements of the living!
By a kind of art the mere names in the churchyard sketch the characters."*

Citing his friend, Walter Del a Mare, he reflects on the ephemeral nature of beauty and the thought that, irrespective of its qualities, it can only be preserved as long as there remains a memory sustain it.

He is referring specifically to countenances, but natural beauty only expresses that quality when it is acknowledged. It requires our interaction with the natural world to make this abstract noun meaningful. Thomas frequent excursions into churches are usually more profane than reverent but the occasional poignancy in his record, like this, suggests he was in fact looking for something deeper than an opportunity to unload his more usual tendency towards derision.

From here he returned across the railway to Cleeve again where the new red brick houses fit only for *"people with immortal souls"* reminded him of the houses he had lived in. He went on the describe a particular house, a Red Brick House in Kent in detail concluding that *"Inside the house a subtle devil was refusing to let a soul enter into its walls"*. The description appears to be, in part, an invention or maybe a composite. It is perhaps closest to Rose Acre Cottage in Bearsted but there is a sense that he is also releasing his frustrations about The Red House near Steep where he was living at this time. The Red House was effectively built for Thomas by Geoffrey Lupton, a devotee of the Arts and Crafts movement. It was a house that neither he nor Helen ever warmed to and this piece was perhaps a way of both expressing and disguising his complaint.

"All other houses that I have known, beautiful, plain, dear, hateful, or dull, have been somehow subdued and made spiritual houses in course of time and of memory. The Red Brick House is the only unconquerable one... Sometimes death will give a soul to a house."

His sojourn through memory and invention continues. It is clear this is going somewhere. *"Sometimes death will give a soul to a house."* As in other works such as 'Light and Twilight', he draws you in. You know it is going somewhere, somewhere uncomfortable, but it is not possible to break free of the narrative. The scene is set with the description of a house with a veranda, its windows shuttered by venetian blinds, its unwelcoming ambience repelling long term tenants *"certainly it had never become a house; it was the corpse, the stillborn corpse of a house."*

The description centres on three children, two older children acting as if in a trance-like state, digging into a sandy bank with spades and a younger child, destressed inconsolably. He captures the feeling of hopelessness when confronted by raw trauma.

"I asked the little girl: " What is the matter with him? "

"He wants his mother," she said.

"Where does he live?" I asked, as I stepped towards the child, meaning to lift him up.

"Over there," she replied, pointing with her eyes to the house of the

verandah".

"Then why doesn't he go home?" I said, stopping still and thinking again chiefly of the house.

"His father is dead," said the little girl and the little boy simultaneously.

"I turned and saw the house looking as if it had grown suddenly old in those few moments — old and haggard, and so cold that I shivered to think how cold it must be in the death-room behind the Venetian blinds."

"As I turned away, the child's sob, the song of the robin, the scream of the swifts, fell into that dark silence without breaking it, like tears into a deep sea... I looked at the house and saw that the soul of the dead man had entered it."

He shifts the mood abruptly to another location and enters an inn. Maybe the sojourn continues, alternatively, if this was a factual account then he probably headed for either the Sloane Hotel or the Queens Arms that faced each other across the Reading Road near Goring and Streatley Railway Station. Neither trade anymore. The Sloane appears to have been converted into flats, the Queens Arms closed in 2014 and is now a Tesco Express.

Thomas describes the Landlord's conversation with a wealthy Masonic Scott and later, two sporting types unable to hold their drink. His disdain is reserved for all parties except the landlord who appears to be able to continue to focus upon his own affairs despite the needful distractions imposed upon him by his customers. With that cameo, Thomas day is concluded.

In his perambulation around the town, Thomas would also have passed the Beehive, the gloriously quaint Catherine Wheel, the John Barleycorn and the Miller of Mansfield in the High Street to name the few that are recorded.

Catherine Wheel, Goring.

[Brakspear Gravity, Boondogle, EPA, Fortyniner]

Quaint outside, heavily timbered inside, large inglenook, part clay pammet floor, fairy lights strung along the beams. It is lightly touched with modern paintwork on the wainscot but then, old photos around the bar stretch back to Thomas time. No sportsmen here today but possibly a Mason.

"Is that a Yorkshire accent" the female bar worker enquires of the Mason.

"I'm a Geordie, we are tighter than Yorkshiremen, ...well I'm not really a Geordie, I come from South Shields."

Showing fake interest "Is that in Liverpool"

Silence.....

I break up this meeting of minds as I look for the gents.

"See the bench, the bench against the wall, that bench, the bench you have just been sitting on!"

"er...yes"

"press the wall next to it."

I look back perplexed

"press the wall next to it"

"er"

"press the wall next to It"

Sufficiently humiliated I comply and without intoning an incantation, without having to bare my breast or left knee the wall miraculously moves aside permitting me access to this male-only inner sanctum. Not the Invisible College, just the Invisible WC. The Geordie looks smug as I leave the premises. He alone is a member of the cognoscenti. He is not quite from far enough north to be a Scott but has all the accoutrements of the Scottish Right. Being as tight as he claimed, maybe he will find a real use for his apron when he attempts to settle his bill at the sink. I trawl through the streets looking for sportsmen but can only find residential care homes.

CHAPTER 5

FIFTH DAY — IVINGHOE TO WATLINGTON ON LOWER ICKNIELD WAY BY ASTON CLINTON, WESTON TURVILLE, CHINNOR AND LEWKNOR

A brief description of the route:

Approximately 25 miles. Thomas returned to Ivinghoe to follow the Lower Icknield Way. On this section of the Way the downs become the feature of the landscape rather than the view from them. Settlements come frequently and most of the route is on what are now predominantly C and B Class roads occasionally interspersed with footpaths and tracks.

***

Ivinghoe

Thomas returned to Ivinghoe, to the dividing of the Ways, this time to follow the Lower Road.

A fresh start on a new leg of the journey. Having undertaken a forty-mile slog the previous day, well according to the narrative at least, mostly through a countryside uninterrupted by human settlement, Thomas narrative once more had a string of villages to break up the dull repetitive descriptions of the roadside verges.

On the old map, the Way enters Ivinghoe past St Mary's Church, the Kings Head and the brewery where *"Some stout and red-faced men stood talking outside the brewery in cheerful mood."*. This was the Roberts and Wilson Brewery at that time. Acquired by Benskins in 1927, the building was demolished in the 1930s. Though no more than a village in 1911, Ivinghoe boasted a Town Hall according to the old map. It was not a centre of local government even when Thomas passed by but is still a hub of community life housing several important functions including a post office and library. Thomas described Ivinghoe as a straggling village with *"many newish houses"*. While these are now *'oldish'*, they have been supplemented by successive generations of incomers. He visited a grocer shop in the village where his sensibilities were challenged by both the sound of a pig being slaughtered next door and the reaction of the locals to this event:

"Neither the shrieking nor the end of it disturbed the stout proprietor cutting up lard and the women talking of the coronation."

This places the timing of this part of Thomas walk in the early summer of 1911, the coronation of George and Mary took place on 22nd June.

Thomas would have passed the Bell a little further along the road which now trades as an Indian. The area between Ivinghoe and Pitstone Green was once adorned with orchards rather than bungalows.

Startop's End

Continuing, Thomas crossed the London North Western Railway reaching the bridge over the Grand Junction Canal about a mile further on where there were two pubs, the White Lion and the Old Queens Head in amongst buildings which *"had the look of canalside and wharfside settlements, a certain squalor more than redeemed by the individuality."* Before Thomas time, the generations of hovels that the poor inhabited would have successively rotted back into the ground. The more substantial parts recycled into other buildings, garden walls or field boundaries even. What endured was a distillation that left the mark of individuality and even in Thomas time was something from another age. The age before mass suburban settlement of *"jerry built rabbit hutches"* that Thomas saw spreading across the land. The cluster of pubs, cottages and canal side paraphernalia is now denuded of the purpose they then had.

The White Lion has been boarded up and left to deteriorate since 2011 and the Old Queens Head has become the Anglers Retreat as if signalling the more leisure-based modern popularity of the canal and the connecting network of reservoirs. As he crossed the canal, he entered Hertfordshire where the road navigates its way around the reservoirs through a series of right-angle turns. By the time he had passed the Wilstone Reservoir, he was back in Buckinghamshire. The Hertfordshire boundary takes the form of a fist punching into Buckinghamshire at this point. Thomas route traversed its mile-wide wrist.

Just beyond this, Thomas came to a road junction that:

"...I shall not forget. The signpost pointed back to Ivinghoe, forward to Aylesbury, Buckland, and Aston Clinton, on the right to Puttenham, on the left to Drayton. There was a small crook to the left before my road went forward again. In the midst of the meeting ways the sign post had a green triangle to stand on. Also, each road had green borders which all widened to the crossing; some of the borders had rushes. The road to Puttenham swelled up a little and fell, and over the rim showed the trees of the vale. Ahead and to the left were the wooded downs."

Now, the Way no longer crooks to the left, the modern B489 has been re-engineered to take precedent. It is the adjoining roads that stagger at this junction now. The triangle of green has gone along with the guidepost. The modern signs direct traffic back to Marsworth, Pitstone, Ivinghoe and Dunstable and ahead to Aylesbury, Tring and Aston Clinton. Only the road to the left is now signed, to Drayton Beauchamp. The wide green borders still widen as they approach the crossroad and the road to Puttenham swells up framing the vale beyond. The wooded downs are still visible to the left. For all that there is nothing in the present junction to arrest the traveller. It is only Thomas description that draws attention to this junction and without that, in its present form, it is unremarkable even at walking pace.

Buckland

Beyond, the road now crosses the A41 dual carriageway in a deep cutting that by-passes Buckland and Aston Clinton. Instead of continuing along the Icknield Way to its junction with Akeman Street Thomas took a diversion into Buckland to visit All Saints church, to seek out the inscriptions on the monuments and found:

"The fleeting moments of Prosperity, the tedious hours of Adversity, and the lingering illness which Providence allotted, she bore with equanimity and Christian resignation...Reader ! Go and do likewise." –

And concluded:

"...one of the most dismal certificates of life, marriage, motherhood, religion, death and the philosophy of relatives that I have seen."

Typically on form with his disdain. In the graveyard outside, he is briefly amused by a headstone for *"Peter Parrot"*.

He passed what he called the 'Bucks Head' in Buckland. The old map, in fact, names the Plough and the Dukes Head either side of the church. Both ceased trading long ago and are now private houses. In the past hundred years this tiny hamlet has become virtually an appendage to the much larger Aston Clinton.

Aston Clinton

Thomas took the backroad from Buckland, through Aston Clinton to Akeman Street passing a *"Rose and Crown, Swan and Palm in Hand"*. Naming three pubs in one village is quite a haul by the standard that Thomas has set so far.

The old map names the Rose and Crown but not the Swan or the Palm in Hand but it does name many others including the Partidge's Arms which he would have passed as he entered the village. The White Lion and the Bell Inn were at the eastern extremity of the village next to the Brewery. He would have passed these had he not taken the diversion through Buckland. The Bull's Arms and the Oak were at the other end of the village, beyond the route he took.

The next illustration, No. 30: *'Aston Clinton'* is sited in Akeman Street looking east towards the White Lion and the Bell with the junction of Twitchell Lane on the left.

A new half tile hung house now sits next to the white rendered house which was the first house on the left in the illustration. The brick house with the window in the gable is either hidden behind the carter in the illustration or is another recent addition to the street. Beyond that now, relatively young trees obscure the terraces towards the end of the street. Despite its village location, the view now looks entirely suburban.

After turning right onto Akeman Street Thomas took the next left along Weston Road. He described the cottages in this street as:

"...a little sordid and all jammed in a row, and three public houses amongst them."

The old map names only the Rothschild Arms and the Waggon and Horses. The Rothschild Arms still trades but as if to make a symbolic statement, a petrol station on the Weston Road, Akeman Street junction has probably replaced the Waggon and Horses. The old map does not reveal the location of the third pub, though the Lost Pub Archive identifies a cottage in the terrace as the Black Horse. In acknowledgement of its history, it is called Black Horse Cottage, there is even a wrought iron hanging sign on its frontage.

The Rothschild Arms, Aston Clinton.

[Doombar]

This pub looked rather different when Thomas passed by, both inside and outside. Old photos on the internet show a more modestly sized pub with just one bay window to the right of the door. The lean-to roof then extended over this and the entrance door alone. This has since been extended over the new bay window to the left of the door and the pub appears to have expanded into the adjoining three-storey property. Outside, in the beer garden, it is another matter. A fantasy beach world complete with sand, beach huts, boats and surfboards. It is here that it reveals itself as a family pub which belies the boozer like face it presents to the main street.

The junction that Thomas could not forget, in its re-engineered form, provides some insight into some of the changes that have been wrought in the past hundred years. Ancient trackways grew out of the landscape or rather, according to Belloc, the indigenous wildlife's interaction with the landscape, humanity playing its own part in the process. Where deliberate construction first began to overlay itself on the primordial network of trackways, it would have been undertaken with local materials. Even in 1911, most of the countryside roads were coloured from the local materials from which they were constructed. The modern blacktops are no longer part of the natural landscape, they stand out from that background, alien in colour and alien in origin. But there is another shift in character that Thomas would have seen only in gestation, management. Legislation that orders the manner in which roads can be used, hardware that orchestrates its everyday use, be that road markings, pedestrian crossings or smart motorways have created a parallel world of motor transport dislocated from the natural world. It is perhaps only adverse weather that can sometimes remind us otherwise. These changes separate Thomas experience of travel from ours, making it unrecoverable.

Some sense of Thomas experience of the countryside can be approximated on a track but even Collins illustrations hint at the change that has been wrought in these too in the past hundred years. The multi-tracked, rutted ways they reveal are indicative of an old working landscape. Each a passage of a cart, seeking ground firm enough to take the load in inclement weather leaves its own mark. It is not worked that way now. The multi-tracks have vanished into a single trackway and in many cases, they have been reduced to little more than a resource for a leisurely stroll. In the rare cases where modern farming horsepower travels off the public highway and is unable to drive the massive pneumatic wheels through the mud regardless, they are often hardened with broken bricks. As is evident from a number of the illustrations in the book, throughout the whole length of the Way there are now but few remnants of the tracks as Thomas would have known them.

~

Weston Turville

Nearly a mile beyond the Rothschild Arms Thomas entered Weston Turville. The road passed through the northern side of the village, with the connecting streets to the south creating a bisected oval of farmland and orchards surrounded by the houses, mills, schools, farms, pubs and churches that comprised the settlement. The neat form of the 1911 version of the village has been compromised. Ribbon and infill development has rendered it into the rather more amorphous, unstructured suburban form of land conveyancing rather than land use.

Thomas lingered in this village. In fact, he appears to have ventured into at least one pub and included one of the most comprehensive lists of pubs in the book.

His meandering around the village is made clear by this list which includes a number of pubs that were off the direct route through the village. *"a Vine, a "Chequers," a "Plough," a "Six Bells," a "Black Horse," a "Chandos," and a "Crown," followed not much beyond the church by a "Marquis of Granby" and a "Swan"*. He even went so far as to describe one of the pubs:

"which had a straight settle facing a curved one of elm with a sloping back and reasonable armrests. There were quoits on pegs under the ceiling, and above the usual circular target for darts; the open fireplace had a kitchen range placed in it. The floor was composed of bluish-black and red tiles alternating."

Rare indeed.

Such a wealth of choice. Of those that traded in 1911, The Plough is now a house, the Chandos Arms still trades, there is a Five Bells in Main Street, the Chequers still trades but the Vine is gone, the Marquis of Granby is now the Village Gate, the Swan appropriately became The End of the World before being demolished.

Could the *"bluish-black and red tiles"* be a clue to the pub name. I gravitated in that direction hoping to be, for once, more definitely on the trail of Thomas choice of pubs.

Checkers, Weston Turvile.

[Doombar, Landlord]

It comes over as the most modest of the remaining pubs in the village, the least extended and upscaled at least. The range and tiled floor could have been in any of the pubs as they were in 1911. There are few if any pubs that have not undergone substantial change over the past hundred years. Whether this was the place that Thomas described is now lost in its layers of archaeology.

A new urban model of living has been developing for some time in the central areas of London and in other major cities. But villages, towns, places like this are left untouched by it. Towns that once had a thriving multi-layered commercial life have faded, the thrall of the suburban lifestyle that has overtaken them since Thomas time still hold these places firmly in its grip. This is what has become of so many places in the past hundred years, settlements stripped of the purpose that created them.

Weston Turville is a sleepy mix of cottages and pubs turned suburban with post-war development. While 'sleepy' is often associated with the archetypical image of county and village life, a place to escape from the city to the lost bucolic England of a previous age, the reality is that it is the suburbanisation of these places that have turned them into sleepy backwaters. When Thomas passed through Weston Turville, as the old map implies, there was still a vibrant rural economy. Now, it is little more than an economically lifeless dormitory and the penultimate stopping off point for the retired. It may claim to have an active social life, but these are things that support a suburban lifestyle not an economy that has any relevance to anything other than the modern fantasy of country life.

You can walk the dogs, go birding, join the golf club and enjoy luxuries unimaginable in a previous age.

This lovely new home is sooo Samantha and Gerry. They have soooo carefully created a beautiful luxury bolt hole out of the wreck of a redundant farm workers cottage. "Yes, we believe he now lives in a care home. It's in a town over thirty-five miles away, thank goodness." "When Gerry is working in London I just keep on top of the potager garden. The herb wheel is a wonder this time of year." "What do I love most about living here?" "It's the way the garage is so cleverly hidden behind the gypsy caravan. I only need to half close my eyes and I can imagine I am living a life like Borrow."

And as we contemplate this month *'things we can't live without'*, has anyone embraced the notion of country life any more self-consciously than those of the present age but understood it less.

~

Thomas speculated that the Way may have left Weston Turville continuing through Stoke Mandeville, Kimblewick, Owlswick and Pitch Green but he chose a more southerly route to Pitch Green through Worlds End, Terrick, Little Kimble and Longwick. The route that is in fact marked on the old map as the Lower Icknield Way.

The Way is now truncated by the A413 a little beyond Worlds End, it requires a quick dash across the carriageway to continue the old route. Next is the bridge under what was the Metropolitan Railway, now Chiltern Railways. Between the two, HS2 is planned to emerge from the Wendover tunnel and plough a furrow across the surrounding fields, cutting across a small plantation and startling the goats. HS2 controversially, will damage not only plantations but 32 Ancient Woodlands. An Ancient Woodland is a wood that has continuously existed since at least 1600. Before that time plantations were uncommon, so anything dating from 1600 is likely to be natural and probably much older. Just to the south of Wendover, Jones Hill Wood is one of the 32. HS2 are committed to plant seven million trees along the route by way of mitigation. Some of this work has commenced. There is little evidence of husbandry in this exercise. Over the course of the 2019 summer, many of the saplings planted as part of this project have died. One farmer estimated that of the 8,000 saplings planted on his land, 6,500 have died. HS2 response can seem rational, they reasoned it would be more efficient to replant the trees that were destined to die than look after them. This moral free, bean counter's view of the world is unarguable in this day and age, so deeply ingrained it has become. The necessary sacrifice of living organisms is *'a price worth paying'* when placed on a bean counter's spreadsheet. Would Thomas agree that our moral compass has not only become distorted but been appropriated by those with little regard for the natural world.

Here the B4009 becomes the A1010 at the Terrick crossroad through a pan flat landscape heading towards Little Kimble.

Little Kimble

The old map names the Crown Inn, it closed in 1999, became an Indian and has since been demolished. Just beyond the Crown the road passes under what was the Aylesbury branch of the Great Western and Great Central Junction Railway, now the Chiltern Railway, a little before Little Kimble Station. Beyond the railway, the road becomes the B4009 again and at the next crossroad the old map indicates the Swan. It still trades in stark white painted brickwork with black windows but was not mentioned by Thomas. The pub faces a long roadside green, beyond this, only the Chilterns that hug the southwestern horizon relieve the flat, rather utilitarian landscape. A ramshackle series of overhead utility wires alongside the green do nothing more than reinforce this utilitarian character.

Longwick

The way continues almost arrow straight, south-west for nearly a mile and a half to Longwick where Thomas mentions the *"Duke of Wellington or Sportsman's Arms"*. Both pubs are named on the old map. They sat at the extremities of a triangular parcel of land which had a Red Lion on the northern apex. The Sportsman is now a filling station, the Duke of Wellington a house but the Red Lion still trades. Immediately beyond the Duke of Wellington the road passed under two branch lines in quick succession. The second now appears to be a cycleway. A mile further on, Thomas left Buckinghamshire and entered Oxfordshire.

Chinnor

At Pitch Green Thomas would have passed the Queen, now converted to cottages in stark black and white reminiscent of the Swan in Little Kimble and on to Chinnor where he left the Way to explore the church. Here, Thomas attention is arrested by a rather gruesome account of a skeleton declaring:

"Here the wicked cease from troubling and the weary are at rest."

None of the settlements Thomas passed through since Weston Turville have changed significantly in size in the past hundred years, Chinnor by contrast has become a significant but largely dormitory settlement of some 6,000. According to the old map, on the way to visit the church Thomas would have passed the Red Lion and on the way back to the main road, the Crown Inn but there were many more pubs in the village that were left unmarked on the old map. Thomas appears to have taken refreshment in at least two.

"At the 'Royal Oak' I listened for half an hour to information and complaints about the heat, which was at the time about ninety degrees [32°C] in the shade, and then went out to make the most of the heat itself..."

Travelling this way today, the temperature reached the unprecedented 35 degrees and I imagined that this was a temperature that Thomas never came close to experiencing. One can always assume too much. The Royal Oak closed in 2011, it was in Lower Road a little past the junction with High Street. He also admits to leaving the Bird in Hand, it was also situated in Lower Road on the junction with Station Road. It closed in 2000.

A little before the perimeter of the post-war housing estate to the west of the village, the blacktopped road turns south leaving a single carriageway continuing south-west for a few hundred yards then a track beyond this for some distance passing north of Kingston Blount and Aston Rowant then crossing the A40 and under the M40 in quick succession and into Lewknor from the north-west along a pleasant single track lane past a manor house, pastoral fields and cottages.

Lewknor

Ye old Leathern Bottel, Lewknor.

There's ponce for you. It was called the Leather Bottle when Thomas passed this way. A quaint timbered pub that still retains two bars. The small one with a large inglenook I take to be what was the public bar by the plain decorations. It has a parquet floor, the only thing that looks a little out of place, a bit 1960's. Otherwise, a place Thomas would have recognised as a pub. It's a Brakspears pub, a beer I first tasted in the early nineties when work brought me in this direction for a few months. It was still brewed in Henley on Thames at that time and to me, seemed a fine ale.

As I was carrying a copy of the next coloured illustration with me, a view of Lewknor showing the pub, I passed it in front of the landlady. She professed little interest commenting only that the church was in the wrong place before seizing upon one of the locals in that hail fellow well met way that gave her an excuse for a quick exit. The local seemed rather taken aback by the unfamiliar attention. I smiled inwardly, thinking, that seems a well placed reaction to my approach. This is my third book and yet I would not call myself a writer or expect anyone to take such a notion seriously. This is partly because I work full time. Much of my spare time, at the moment, is spent building an extension to my home, more on the normal domestic duties present in any modern relationship. Hoovering the floor, emptying and filling the dishwasher and washing machine, cleaning the toilet, doing the shopping. Sometimes I watch television, when I've no energy left to do anything else. In the leftover moments, I attempt to write. Sometimes I make real progress but it seems just as often that I sit in front of the PC and after a few minutes realise that I am too tired to get the brain into gear. Sometimes I resort to reading through the text and maybe achieve no more than changing the odd word or punctuation mark or two. It is slow progress. Anyone who has attempted this kind of thing will know that there are those moments of inspiration when the sense of a theme distils unexpectedly out of the aether. The inspiration can seem unforgettable, but then you do. Occasionally the idea comes back to you, sometimes I have the presence of mind to scribble something down on a scrap of paper, occasionally I'm organised enough to have a notebook to hand. However this transpires, the words I finally get onto the written page are by varying degrees only a pale shadow of the original inspiration. Then of course, there are those times when you pick up a book and are astounded at the art and craftsmanship of another. Even though I only read non-fiction these days, there are many moments like that. To write is one thing, to be a writer is another. Then there are those moments of astonishment when, having spent days writing paragraphs in the attempt to express an idea, then editing them over and over and .....finally it crystallises into just half a dozen words. These moments are rare but that is not all. Next comes the bodging.

Once the narrative is complete, it needs to be formatted into a book. I can only accept a limited amount of white space at the bottom of a page. Bodging is the activity of adding redundant text into the finished narrative to reduce the white space and ensure that illustrations fit neatly onto the page. This whole thing is a shamelessly amateur endeavour.

LEWKNOR

The illustration shows the gable end of the pub from the far side of the High Street looking northeast towards the church. The church has simply been hidden behind the modern stand of trees. That apart, little has changed other than the blacktop road surface, the cars in the car park, the loss of a grand elm and the ubiquitous Mediterranean sunshades in the garden.

The roads to the south of Lewknor have been reconstructed since Thomas time, probably partly occasioned by the construction of the M40 which passes within a whisker of the village. The B4009 Watlington Road now bypasses the village, its former route truncated by the M40. Watlington Road now re-joins the B4009 to the west of the village at a 'T' junction. The road continues roughly to the south-west through Shirburn to Watlington.

Watlington.

Watlington was a small market town that is only a little larger than the one Thomas passed through. The narrow streets through this un by-passed town present a series of bottlenecks to motorised traffic.

Thomas did not seem that impressed by Watlington, describing it as *"a big square village of no great beauty or extraordinary antiquity, all of a piece and rustic... there is no market at Watlington"*. Sometimes his knowledge, or is it his natural bent for cynicism, lets him down. In fact, Watlington is, or at least was, a market town with indications of settlement going back to the 6th century. Despite Thomas dismissive assessment, the illustrator included two illustrations in his book.

The first is unmistakable, No. 31: *'Watlington Town Hall'*. Little has changed apart from the vehicular bottleneck and the shopfronts on the left.

The box planters seem to be a poor attempt to disguise the way this building has been robbed of its 'groundedness'

As I walked around the town looking for the location of the second illustration, I was approached by an older gent looking as if to help. I did not notice the white stick he carried at first and offered him a copy of the illustration. He was partially sighted rather than blind but he was unable to identify the location from the small copy. We chatted for a while discussing the various qualities of the remaining pubs in the town. A subject he took a keen interest in. Particularly the relationship between the town's pubs and the Hayward family who seemed to be intent on establishing a monopoly interest in them in the eighteenth century. He recommended the Carriers Arms as it was the only pub not tied to Brakspears, a brew he considered to be Thames bilge water. Familiarity breeds... as they say.

I tried to take him up on his recommendation, but it was closed.

I found the site of the next illustration along Brook Street, No. 32: *'Watlington'*. It looks east towards Watlington Hill.

Apart from the risks associated with standing in the middle of the road in the attempt to replicate the illustration and the loss of the pubs, little has changed.

Watlington now has that rather 'polite', comfortable middle class feel that is often reflected in more prosperous settlements. It is the rather insular economic life of home keeping. With its designer lifestyle shops, a kitchen shop, a Scandi shop, a chocolatier, a boutique bike shop, a deli/café, even the charity shop is a boutique charity shop. This home to Sky News correspondents offers everyday comforts and indulgences that Thomas and Helen only experienced as a rare gift from more wealthy friends.

A story of loss and change is told by the buildings that cluster around the village centre that betray their former life as pubs. A walk around the central block alone revealed the Barley Mow, Black Horse, Royal Oak, Hare and Hounds and the Three Tuns. When Thomas visited, according to the lost pubs archive, he had the choice of over ten pubs. He stayed overnight in one. It had a rather unique facility. His room was hung with pictures, so much so that he described it as a picture gallery and included a detailed description of it in his narrative.

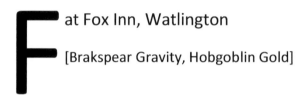

F at Fox Inn, Watlington

[Brakspear Gravity, Hobgoblin Gold]

It was called the Fox and Hounds in 1911. There is nothing about the place to suggest that this was the pub Thomas stayed in, it is simply one of the few pubs still trading.

There was a travelling fair in the town when Thomas visited. He retreated to a taproom to escape the steam-driven noise. He spent the night in the inn and ended the day with a diatribe describing the paintings on the walls of his bedroom, applying his well honed critical skills to popular romantic art, spiced up with overtones of his customary sarcasm. It is difficult to be sure whether this episode is not just a page filler, a reflection of his mood, some meaningful contribution to the narrative or just a recollection and identification with the visionary effects of the laudanum use of his youth. Perhaps it also betrays, in a visual arts form, his rejection of romantic and visionary poetry. Symbolically, a turning point away from that form of representational art towards the more naturalistic metre crystallised through his conversations with Robert Frost a couple of years later.

I have tried to identify some of the paintings from Thomas description but to no avail. After trawling through Google Images several times, fruitlessly, I thought the National Gallery might be able to help and sent them a copy of Thomas descriptions. I was fobbed off by return in no uncertain terms.

~

CHAPTER 6
SIXTH DAY — WATLINGTON TO UPTON BY EWELME, WALLINGFORD, LITTLE STOKE, THE PAPIST WAY, LOLLINGTON AND BLEWBURY

A brief description of the route:

About 15 miles, much of this day sees Thomas walking speculatively, attempting to find evidence of the Way and alternative river crossings beyond Watlington on footpaths, roads and trackways and their possible association with the more ancient routes he was attempting to recover.

***

"For supper, bed, and picture gallery my host at Watlington charged me two shillings, and called me at five into the bargain, as I wished to breakfast at Wallingford. I took the turning to Ewelme out of the Oxford road, and was soon high up among large, low-hedged fields of undulating arable"

Thomas left Watlington on the B4009 heading south-west through another arable landscape of huge skies and distant horizons. In a little over a mile, he was passing Britwell Priory and entering the edge of the diminutive village of Britwell Salome.

Britwell Salome

"The village was scattered among trees, not interrupting the smell of hay. The road skirted it, and was soon out again amongst the wheat, and passing Britwell park, where the cattle were crossing in a straight line between groups of elms. In the hedge there was bracken along with the yellow bedstraw and white bryony. For a time there were gorse and bracken together on the green strip above the road."

This unremarkable passage is typical of many of Thomas narrative descriptions. They are a pale shadow of the descriptive powers he commands in his other works and are easily hurried past, but when read quietly and slowly they reveal the shadow of another England. One can sometimes feel the simple grace and lost beauty through his words, words that have now become much harder to write with the same simple honesty. The sounds, the smells, the anxieties of a world Thomas never got to know now bear down on such a scene and strip it of the imagined innocence we read into it.

For such a small settlement it comes as a surprise that Thomas was able to name two pubs here, the Plough and the Sun. The old map does not indicate either of them but it does name the Red Lion which still trades.

Thomas turned left off the B4009 about a mile beyond Britwell Salome, south towards Ewelme on an unclassified road which he did not consider to be a part of the Icknield Way. He was seeking or at least thinking about alternative crossing points on the Thames.

Ewelme

Ewelme was a substantial if stretched and scattered village when Thomas passed through. It has grown very little in the past hundred years and retains a rustic charm which is enhanced by the topography as it drops down into the shallow valley which encloses a series of ponds, watercourses and watercress beds.

He visited St Mary's Church, so often his way and though he could not get in, a memorial on a tombstone outside inspired Thomas to reflect on the paintings he had deconstructed the previous evening and led him on to despise their sentiments and the *"Kind angels and dust"* in the verse on Alice Heath's tomb in a similar manner. By the east window he found an inscription much closer to his liking:

"Here lyeth the Body of Margaret Machen who departed this life the sixth of April being aged 20 years"

Anno Dom. 1675.

This simple, unsentimental inscription marking the premature end of a young person's life two hundred years previously needed, in Thomas view, no sentimental overtures to make clear its essential poignancy. Here we are suddenly closer to Thomas, the irritation, impatience and disdain that underlies so much of his cynicism and sarcasm, his diatribes and bloody-minded anger stripped away when confronted by such simple, unadorned frankness.

From the church, Thomas headed down Burrows Hill passing near the Greyhound which he mentioned. The old map shows the Greyhound and the Shepherds Hut. The latter was a beer house. It was off his route and towards the west end of the village. It still trades but the Greyhound has long since become a private house.

Thomas headed out of the village past a series of low slung farm buildings lining the slightly hollowed Day's Lane and out into the initially unhedged road beyond with its clear views across Cow Common and the downs beyond.

The road crossed what was then the Benson-Dorchester Road. Now, that way to Benson has been truncated by the runway of RAF Benson. A WW2 legacy, now home to helicopter squadrons. He crossed the road into Clacks Lane, sharing the road with the Upper Icknield Way for a few yards again before they parted as Clacks Lane veered off almost due west towards Crowmarsh Gifford.

Crowmarsh Gifford

Thomas continued west along what was then Marsh Lane. This route has now been disrupted by the intervention of the A4074 bypassing Wallingford.

"Crowmarsh is a wide street of old cottages leading to Wallingford bridge"

A defuse, one street settlement in 1911, it is now substantially tighter packed and looks even more like a satellite of Wallingford than it did then. The Queens Head Inn still trades opposite the junction at which Thomas turned right towards Wallingford Bridge.

Crowmarsh ends as the bridge begins, the Thameside parkland around the eastern approach to the bridge forming just a visual break. Wallingford begins immediately after the bridge.

Wallingford

"I crossed the bridge to the town, and went up the narrow, old street, past an inn called "The Shakespeare," to the small square of small shops, where red and blue implements of farming stood by the pillared town hall and the sun poured on them."

Wallingford was a substantial market town in 1911. The old map indicated a PH and two Inns in the High Street, an Inn and a PH in St Leonards Lane, an Inn and three PH's in St Mary's Street, a PH in Station Road – there must have been many more, unmarked.

In this same area now is the Boat House, the Town Arms and the George in the High Street; the Dolphin, the Green Tree and the Coachmakers Arms in the area around Market Square; the Coach and Horses, the Partridge and the Cross Keys further out.

The bridge is the site of the next illustration, No. 33: 'Wallingford Bridge'.

In this view, surprisingly little has changed. Perhaps I should not have waited for a gap in the traffic, it gives a false impression.

There is a long list of pubs that have closed since Thomas visit in 1911. The Shakespeare in the High Street closed in 1913, the Beehive in the High Street closed in 1976, the Hope and Anchor in the High Street closed in 1916, the Lamb in the High Street closed in 1960, the Red Lion Hotel in High Street closed in 1940, the Fat Ox in Hart Street closed in 1940, the Feathers in St Martins Street closed in 1959, the French Horn in Church Lane closed in 1911, the Greyhound in St Johns Road closed in 1950, the Plough in St Johns Road closed in 1996, the Ironmongers Arms in Market Place closed in 1914, the Kings Head in Market Place closed in 1920, the Little House on the Corner by the Brook in St Leonards Way closed in 1996, The Anchor in St Leonards Lane closed in 1940, the Royal in St Marys Street closed in 2008, the White Hart in St Marys Street closed in 1962, the Waggon and Horses in Goldsmiths Lane closed in 1927.

"I went into the 'private bar' of an inn, but hearing only a bluebottle and seeing little but a polished table, and smelling nothing else, I went out and round the corner to the taproom of the same inn. Here there were men, politics, crops, beer, and shag tobacco."

The choice of pubs in this town now pales into insignificance to the choice of pubs Thomas had in 1911. Consequently, by the normal rules of chance, the likelihood of the pub Thomas used being one of those that still trades is very low. Whichever it was, it was able to inspire a mid-day diatribe about The Jolly Drover in Coldiston.

I walked around the town looking for a pub that might have had a private bar, past the town hall that now, in keeping with the times, is a tourist centre rather than a trading place for farm implements. But the marketplace that Thomas knew has been more or less hollowed out of pubs. Just the Dolphin and Green Tree remain. Today the Dolphin is a basic boozer with one bar, not quite a taproom but....

D

olphin, Wallingford.

[Morlands Bitter, Rev James, The Dolly, IPA, Robinsons Unicorn]

On the walls are a number of antique framed Schweppes adverts for table water, ginger ale, soda water and the like, all endorsed by raven or red-headed ladies of romance. The display has echoes of Thomas bedroom gallery. They look as though they would only be comfortable one of Coldistons Hotels rather than its taprooms.

The Jolly Drover in Coldiston is in fact a satire. These seemingly out of place diatribes can be quickly rushed past by the reader but they are always revealing. In this one Thomas pulls no punches in a particularly insightful and ultimately brutal manner. He was not averse to poking fun at all classes in his Chaucerian descriptions of people as we will see a little further into today's journey, his contempt however was reserved for a particular type. I wonder how many of his modern day admirers actually get this.

He describes, through the analogy of the private bar facing the towns fine streets and the taproom facing a small corner of wasteland, two worlds, not in collision but moving separately, sharing no empathy or even comprehension of the dynamic of the others life. One sensing the disdain felt towards them by 'polite society':

"Look at them staring at us as if we were wild beasts taking an airing outside the cage."

The other affirming this:

*"Where do they come from? Of course they do not live in Coldiston:
then why come here to drink? They cannot, of course, be stuffed into
prison or workhouse or asylum; but is there no other cesspool possible in
an age with a genius for sanitation?"*

The whole episode is Thomas invention, one through which he makes a
personal and unambiguous statement. In drawing its conclusion, he leaves
no doubt where his sympathies lie. Attempts to bridge the gap between
these two worlds are usually deferred to the same prejudiced self-interest
that Thomas observed.

"It is extraordinary, they [polite society] *think as they pass by the
turning down to the Tap, how a lot of lazy fellows, with nothing to do and
with only rags on them, can get enough to spend half a day there. That
ought certainly not to be allowed...But when there are half a dozen rough
men and women talking aloud and gesticulating like foreigners over the
price of a long, brown dog that shivers under a cart, they do not see why it
should be so"*

And as if from today's hymn sheet,

*"These are not the honest poor. Either a man must work, or be looking
out for work in a serious manner, or be so well dressed that he obviously
need not work; or something is wrong."*

Perplexed by the sight of a tall man from that other world standing at the
bar in the taproom, cutting a dignified air, one of Coldiston's 'worthies' is
irritated by the very sight of such impudence. His own paltry character is
exposed by this unfortunate comparison. He takes vengeance by
scapegoating his wife then weakly turns to her for comfort. He finds none,
Thomas clearly considering him worthy of nothing but ignominy.

Setting aside British Society's enduring ability to wilfully stigmatise the
lower classes, the undertow of this tale, the shadow lurking in its
background is also Thomas own preoccupations and limited capacity to deal
with life's difficulties. Referring wistfully to the tall, dignified customer in

the taproom:

"He is not thinking about rent, accounts, education, clothes, the poor, church, chapel, appendicitis, or this time next year. He is not apparently in a hurry. He has no vote, and one party in power is as good as the other to him."

Words that could just as well be ruefully stated by Thomas himself when in a Borrovian frame of mind.

~

Thomas returned to the east bank of the river following a track then called Watery Lane, over Grims Ditch, where the A4130 now forms a new river crossing as it bypasses the town to the south. He continued south past Mongwell, beyond North Stoke to Little Stoke House where there was a ferry crossing some three miles downstream from Wallingford.

Cholsey

Here he crossed the river, continuing along a track heading west towards Cholsey. It became the Papist Way, according to the old map, beyond what is now the A329 Reading Road. The settlement of Cholsey was still some way off in 1911. The old map shows just a couple of isolated terraces and the Star Inn hinting at the village beyond. According to Thomas, the pub was called the Morning Star and indeed it still trades with this name. As he passed, *"They were talking about roads"*

Thomas paused here to list a series of not too flattering vignettes of the customers. The fat drayman, the needy cyclist, the foreign-looking chauffeur, the man with big red ears who appreciated the value of garden flowers because they had a price, over wayside plants which did not. With all the characteristics of a taproom, I discovered belatedly, that the Morning Star is no longer a pub of the regular kind.

M orning Star, Cholsey.

Visually it is still a basic boozer but is in fact the home of the Fair Mile Sports and Social Club. This had not registered when I entered the premises. There was a distracted air about the place as several people were engaged in the preparations for a celebratory social event that evening. Banners, decorations and balloons festooned the beer garden. As I approached the bar, seeming surprised to see me, the barman asked, 'how was I doing'. It was a hot day on the road, and in need of a drink I replied, 'it's been a bit of a struggle'. He served a beer and returned to his duties elsewhere.

I was left alone in the bar, found a seat and slowly took in the surroundings. There on the wall was a sign indicating that 'non-members were required to contribute £1 towards temporary membership'. I realised that the Morning Star was no longer a pub but a private members club and a rather neat way of saving an old pub, an old taproom, for posterity. Clearly, the landlord, if that is still an appropriated title in an establishment of this kind, assessed my need humanely and waived the normal formalities. I finished the beer; everyone was still preoccupied with their preparations, so I deposited a couple of quid in the RNLI box on the end of the bar before I departed.

~

A little further on, beyond the junction where the Railway Hotel once stood, Thomas turned to the south under what was the Great Western Railway along a track and then path that turned west before Lollingdon Hill. It continued past Lollingdon Farm, the site of the next illustration, No. 34: *'By Lollingdon Farm'*.

The site of the illustration is just beyond the farm looking back towards the east. The *"many thatched farm buildings"* that Thomas described are now hard to find. According to the illustration at least, most seemed to have been plain tiled with bonnet hip tiles then and now. The one clearly thatched building in the illustration has been partly demolished. The retained remainder is now sheeted in asbestos.

Continuing west, Thomas approached the Astons', Tirrold and Upthorpe via West End.

Aston Tirrold and Aston Upthorpe

According to the old map, the Tirrold's were then immersed in orchards and as Thomas observed *"from the east it seemed all trees and orchards"*. The modern development that has filled the vacuum left by the orchards has effectively joined the two villages into a single settlement without disturbing its quaintness.

Thomas walked around the villages, attempted to visit Aston Tirrold Church, which was locked and mocked Aston Upthorpe's church spire as *"stupid"*. He described the villages as:

"...here you pass a mud wall, there a hedge, here boarded, there thatched and again a tiled cottage."

This description remains reasonably accurate even now despite the more uniform post-war infill. According to the old map, walking around the village, Thomas could have passed the Checkers Inn and the Boot Inn. The Checkers is now the Fat Frog in the Checkers. The Boot Inn has been rebuilt as a far more substantial building than the one Thomas may have passed. It is now in residential use.

Thomas continued on a track just to the south of Blewburton Hill towards Blewbury.

Blewbury

Thomas described Blewbury as a village much like the Astons, similarly immersed in orchards. However, on what was the main road to Wantage, it benefited from many more pubs.

Thomas lists a series of pubs that were along what was then London Street, now London Road. The Barley Mow, Catherine Wheel, George and Dragon, Sawyers Arms, Load of Mischief and the New Inn. Deeper into the village there was a Red Lion. You read these names and feel that something vital has been lost from our lives, our culture, and our purpose. The Red Lion still trades and what was the Barley Mow is the rebuilt Blueberry. The rest have gone.

Thomas was particularly taken with the Load of Mischief which was a few doors along South Street. It is now a house. He was glad to see an advertisement for 'Votes for Women' and the Hogarth type pub sign of a *"magnificent...huge, lusty, brown virago"* holding a bottle of gin mounted on the shoulders of her *"ill-chosen spouse"*.

"...It did not assert anything more than that a big, gin drinking woman on a small man's shoulders was a 'load of mischief"

Thomas considered the irony that such a woman was considered a load of mischief and yet the man that brewed the gin and grew rich on the proceeds became a justice of the peace or a member of parliament.

"...it is the difference between mind and matter, between brain-work and manual labour...a history of England was once written entirely to show this difference, to insist upon it...a Guide to Tuft-hunting, Sycophancy, Boot-licking and other services to the Aristocracy and Plutocracy and to Keeping in Your Place."

While the book title may be an invention, the sentiments are all Thomas. Thomas went into the taproom of one of the pubs. He did not name it but it is hard to imagine that it was not the Load of Mischief. As if by design, he shared it with a beer-drinking *"...shrill and lean, large eyed woman of middle age somewhat in liquor"* who had predicted that it would not rain that day. It began to rain soon after she left but in demonstration of the natural order of things rather than man's artificial hierarchies it fell *"...upon her, as it did upon the roofs, mackintoshes and umbrellas of the brewers, publicans and brewery shareholders."*

Load of Mischief, now a house,

Upton

Thomas followed the road through Blewbury north-west for about a mile to Upton. Then, Upton was little more than a hamlet, again immersed in orchards. He pursued his course no further that day but returned for his overnight stop to one of the six inns in Blewbury and embarked instead on an episode of literary criticism inspired by the book he carried with him. James Montgomery's Pelican Island. A poem that he speculated was *"carried on under the influence of an ecstasy given to the author by an explorer's book"*. The explorer was Captain Matthew Flinders, his book, the 'Voyage to Terra Australis'

The Barley Mow, Blewbury.

[West Berkshire Brewery Good Old Boy, Tribute]

Today the choice of pubs is rather more limited than when Thomas passed this way. This modern iteration of the Barley Mow is something between a local and a road pub. Many of the pubs Thomas passed were road pubs in their day but that name seems to imply something quite different now.

The sound of conversation is coming from all quarters, music is playing over the sound system but is virtually inaudible and a TV is silently showing Sky Sport. No one is watching it. Well, I'm watching it, abstractly. Tennis. I dishonestly feign interest to disguise myself.

Born in the late, middle eighteen hundreds, died early in the last century, living all his life in the last millennium there is one further measure that is more significant to Thomas life than any of the above. The industrialisation of the country was an established fact in Thomas lifetime, the encroachment of an industrial scale of urban and suburban development into the countryside something he was all too aware of. Agriculture too had been changing for at least a century but had yet to scale up to anything like the agribusiness of the modern age. The countryside probably seemed a far more secure sanctuary to Thomas then, than it would now.

Something more significant than any of this has transpired only in the last few years. We have undergone a transition from the Holocene geological epoch to the Anthropocene, such has been the impact of industrialised humanity since the end of the second world war. Geological epochs have always been the work of millennia. The Jurassic epoch lasted 55 million years, the Cretaceous 75 million years, following on from the great extinction that brought the end of the giant lizards, the Tertiary lasted 62 million years, the Holocene, the epoch in which Thomas lived covers only 11,700 years. It seems something has brought it to its end astonishingly prematurely. We are moving with unprecedented speed into the Anthropocene. The epoch defined entirely by the impact of humanity on the planet, on its geological strata. We know the litany, our sins against nature. Enhanced $Co2$ concentrations, plastics, nitrogen and phosphorous fertilisers, airborne particulates and radioactive isotopes are laying down their sediments in the geological bedrock being created by the modern world. Then alongside this, the 'Silent Spring'. It is projected that the sixth mass extinction that is currently in process will see the elimination of 75% of all life on earth within just the next few centuries. And all this in the few short years since Thomas death in Arras.

In this context, Thomas choice of reading material is illuminating. It takes an act of cognitive dissonance to disregard the difference of even Thomas perception of Australia to that of the modern age. The Ashes, the Opera House , the Sidney Harbour Bridge, A Town Like Alice are so grounded in the modern consciousness even to those that have never visited the place, yet in 1911 Thomas was born within a couple of generations of those that had, like Mathew Flinders, just began the process of exploration.

Happening upon a virgin land then untouched by western culture, by industrialised humanity. still *"a manless Eden"* Mathew Flinders, the explorer and inspiration, James Montgomery the visionary could experience and in turn articulate an uncontaminated world where a pristine nature carried on an unsullied life, unconsciously, in a way that is all but unimaginable to anyone in this present age,

"Whether it was through the impulse of the discoverer's words, or, as is more likely, through his own nature, he was able to suggest with some power the world that does without men."

Maybe we are on the cusp, just. But those yet to be born in the Anthropocene epoch that presently unfolds will know even less of this. These visions, this poetry will bring no comfort to those whose lives will be bereft of that kind of experience.

The tragic irony is that the exploration of a virgin land is only ever a prelude to its exploitation and the ruin of the indigenous cultures.

~

CHAPTER 7
SEVENTH DAY — STREATLEY TO SPARSHOLT ON THE RIDGEWAY BY SCUTCHAMER KNOB AND LETCOMBE CASTLE

A brief description of the route:

About 20 miles. Thomas returned to Streatley, this time with the intention of following the Ridgeway, not because he considered it to be a miss named section of the Icknield Way but just for the pleasure of following it. It was a walk of unique character, climbing rapidly from the Thames Riverside up to the peaks of the Ridgeway hills. An open countryside of usually unhedged trackways with little in the way of settlements to pass through.

***

Streatley

At some point in his visits to both Goring and Streatley, Thomas would have crossed the bridge that links the two places. Topographically they mark the punctuation between the downs of the Chilterns and the downs of the Ridgeway. The bridge, the means of traversing this transition.

The bridge was the site on another illustration that I have placed here. There is an equally strong case to have included it in his day 4 travels, No. 35: *'The Bridge at Goring'*. The bridge was reconstructed in 1923 in a form that attempted to reflect the style of the original timber bridge.

Wider, stronger and thereby able to carry what was considered modern traffic in 1923, the bridge still fits seamlessly into the adjoining road network nearly a hundred years later, now straddling the gap between a park-like landscape and a tree-clad island rather than the waste suggested in Collins illustration.

The seventh day begins back in Streatley. From here, Thomas set out to follow the Ridgeway *"chiefly because I like the Ridgeway"* and this, despite having concluded that the reference to it being the Icknield Way on the old maps was misplaced. From the Bull Hotel Thomas followed what is now the A417 north then west on a narrow C Class road past a series of *"red spots"*, the new houses that were claiming not only Cleve but this road too as it escapes the Thames flood plain towards the higher land of the chalk downs.

Climbing steadily past the golf club the Way reaches the site of the next illustration, No. 36: *'Ridgeway near Streatley'*. It appears to have been taken just beyond the golf club looking west in an area that is now obscured by trees and shrubs and colonised by yet more *"red spots"*.

The view along Thurle Down is now only visible beyond the roadside tree line, in the adjacent fields.

About three-quarters of a mile beyond the golf club and at about 300 feet, the blacktop gives way to an unsurfaced track and the start of a steeper accent to 600 feet.

Thomas notes a junction crossing the track with what he describes as the roads to *"Aldworth and Compton on the left, Cholsey and Wallingford on the right."* They may have been roads by 1911 standards but these tracks could hardly have changed and today, are more suited to walking, riding or 4x4's. The presence of a guidepost at this junction as indicated on the old map suggests that these tracks had a more important status then. The only guidepost now just indicates that this is the Ridgeway while other signs state that motorised vehicles are prohibited between October and April.

From here, the Way begins to descend slowly but despite this, as it crosses over the tops of the downs it feels like it is on the roof of the world with huge skies and distant horizons or as Thomas says:

"It was as free as the blue paths in the snowy heavens. It looked down upon everything but the clouds..."

The descent is arrested on the line of the disused Didcot, Newbury and Southampton Railway, now just a treeline in the otherwise open landscape. Remarkably, just to the north, in a thickening of the trees, stood the remote Churn Station. Accessed only by unmetalled sheep tracks, there is nothing but fields for miles around and so it was in 1911 according to the old map. Remarkably, the station only closed in 1962, and the line it was served by in 1966.

The track begins to ascend once more, then takes a sharp right-hand turn well before East Ilsley as if some repelling magnetism is driving the Way clear of any settlement. Within this crook in the track the old map indicates a pavilion in the fields of Compton Downs and according to Thomas:

"Before it was ordained that cricket should be played on billiard tables, there were a pitch and a pavilion here beside the Ridgeway near the Abingdon road. Elevens drove up from Oxford, and a cheerful scene it was..."

In the heady environment of this wide-open dome of sky he drifts on into one of his mid-day reveries, beginning by comparing this singular...

"...morning rendezvous for men with lurchers after the hares, a refuge for belated soldiers, a convenience for several breeds of idlers, philosophers, and adventurers... it was the nearest approach to a permanent hermitage on the ridge of these downs."

...to the only remaining permanent hermitage on the downs; Wayland's Smithy. In this environment, it is not hard to imagine Thomas drifting across this landscape lost in the meditative stream of consciousness to come.

This stream of consciousness begins with his remarkably modern sounding scathing assessment of the moral compass of the press and the publics wanton reactions to their inventions, then continues with a long harrowing tale of the fate of Arthur Aubrey Bishopstone who had taken refuge in the wayside Lone Barn with his wife and six children just before Christmas. Thomas describes the barn. He claims to have visited it and the fine detail of his description makes this seem real. In amongst the fallen debris of the decaying building he chanced upon a pocketbook. *"On the front page was written, A. A. Bishopstone, College, Oxford, October, 1890."* The tale that follows is probably all Thomas invention or maybe based on some facts with perhaps the names, locations and details changed. Though, that aside, there seems to be too much of Thomas in it for it to be anything but a judgement upon himself.

On Christmas Day a seventh child was born to the Bishopstone's. Following a visit from a doctor, aghast at the conditions in which they were living, Arthur Aubrey Bishopstone was arrested and his wife and children were taken to the workhouse. Thomas transcribes a series of harrowing quotations taken from Bishopstone's supposed journal. They could equally have been transcribed from Thomas own journals, written on his many walks in the countryside, an expression of the tortured melancholy he grappled with on them. Typically:

"We are looking for straight oak sticks in a world where it is hazel that grows straight."

And

"What is man ? One moment he is a prayer, another a flower of God, another a flame to consume he knows not what save that it is himself..."

A man lost in the imponderables of existence and rendered incapable of undertaking his duties to his family. But it is in the mouths of others that he attempts to place the final judgement about himself:

"Francis Albert Edward, born at Lone Barn on Christmas Day, recovered from the effects of his birth and left the workhouse at the end of June with his mother and four brothers. I believe that after Lone Barn there was nothing they missed less than Arthur Aubrey Bishopstone. If they had been given to considering such matters, they would have said that he ought to have lived [alone]..."

Again, the word philosopher comes up during this reverie. This is not Thomas claiming, taking on the mantle of philosopher. Real or imagined, these encounters reveal Thomas own inner life, a higher intellect, we might say a higher self is explaining these matters to the mortal man.

There is no evidence of a Lone Barn here on the old map though interestingly, he would indeed have passed a Lone Barn near Charing on his walks along the Pilgrims Way with Harry Hooton.

Continuing along a gentle rise and heading north-west, the track reaches 550 feet at what Thomas described as the Abingdon Road, the A34 dual carriageway now carves its way across the landscape.

Beyond, the Way continues, now following and occasionally entangling with Grimes Ditch to the north and steadily rising to well over 600 feet at Scutchamer Knob Plantation or as Thomas suggests, Scotchman's Hob. At the crossing of the B4494 above Wantage it reaches 700 feet.

Continuing on the other side it shares a blacktop surface briefly before returning to a track to *"places suited for exploring the ridges and solitudes of the spirit"* reaching 750 feet amongst the Tumuli of Lattin Down.

The way continues west taking a crook to the left then right on a blacktop farm track to the crossing with the A338 Wantage Road. It crooks back to the right then quickly to the left on this section of road:

"Probably the half a mile or more between the two crooks is not an innovation, but the crooks themselves are, as it were, the punishment inflicted on the old road by two newer or at some time more vigorous roads cutting across it."

Continuing west, the Way skirts past the southern edge of Letcombe Castle and the site of the next illustration, No. 37: *'Letcombe Castle'*.

The site of the illustration is from the eastern section of the earthwork nearest the Ridgeway looking along the ditch to the west. It's a familiar sight, the earthwork now inundated with trees and shrubs, filling the ditch and lining the tops. Like so many of the illustrations in the book, the East Anglian Dykes, Wandleberry, Whitecross and now Letcombe; they have been let go sometime in the last hundred years and are being reclaimed by a nature.

Nearby is the site of the next colour illustration *'From the Ridgeway above Wantage'* looking south over Letcombe Basset and Letcombe Regis towards Wantage:

FROM THE RIDGEWAY ABOVE WANTAGE.

and by contrast, hardly changed.

The Way continues as a wide, sky hugging turf track past Folly Clump, a name Thomas objects to. The use of the word 'Folly' he considered to be a form of condemnation of the extraordinary by those with a conventional limited vision, those who would seek to suppress and control nature and the march of history by inventing a pastiche to replace it. Prophetic.

The Way skirts around Hackpen Hill and the Devils Punchbowl and crosses the B4001 at Sparsholt Firs at which point it becomes a blacktop road again for a short distance before peeling away, this time onto a metaled road in the form that Thomas would have recognised and continues to rise to nearly 800 feet. The metaled road soon fades back into a turf track. Near Blowingstone Hill Thomas left the way and headed down what is now a C Class, single-track road into Sparsholt.

"Down from the realm-long bridge of islands above the world the traveller descends into cities of men".

He does not record the location of his overnight accommodation, but the old map indicates the Star beerhouse in this tiny settlement set amongst orchards. It still trades.

Sparsholt

The Star, Sparsholt.

[Doombar, Proper Job]

There is no evidence that Thomas spent the night here. He is just as likely to have called into a cottage to see if they could *"spare a bed"*. Such intrusions into privacy did not seem to be out of place back then. In 1911 country folk were probably grateful for the opportunity to earn a couple of extra shillings but such country folk no longer live in these cottages.

The Star now has 4 AA stars, well above Thomas price range. It is an old, banded brick and stone building that has been knocked through inside into a single floorplate. It retains a wooden boarded floor, a low slung timber ceiling but is light, bright and modern in all other respects. Most tables are set out with wine glasses as well as cutlery, it seems to be run by a charming French lady. Comfortable leather sofas provide a relaxed and spacious sitting area for those just drinking – soft music plays unobtrusively, allowing my mind to drift...

Odd that in an environment I have responded too so positively, I should drift towards negatively. Maybe I have been spending too much time with Thomas. Well within the span of the past hundred years our awareness of the natural world has changed. In the past fifty years in particular, natural history broadcasting has created a far larger and more sophisticated audience with an awareness of the issues of habitat destruction, species extinction and climate change. More people turn self consciously to the countryside as a resource for wellbeing and inspiration than ever. What can we do, pick up litter, clear out a pond. Despite this progress, what does weekend volunteering accomplish, really. Something must be done – we know that and we delude ourselves that our small contributions are meaningful, but are they. We carry the burden of a Helpless Knowledge. We know we are on the wrong course, that something must be done but there is so much that is set against our puny efforts. This fact is nothing new. To quote a nineteenth-century French seer, Frederic Bastiat, on the subject of the enduring economic and political organisation constructed by society's elites:

"When plunder becomes a way of life, men create for themselves a legal system that authorises it and a moral code that glorifies it"

CHAPTER 8
EIGHTH DAY — SPARSHOLT TO TOTTERDOWN ON THE RIDGEWAY, BY WHITE HORSE HILL AND WAYLAND'S SMITHY

A brief description of the route:

About 10 miles. Thomas returned to the Ridgway heights to continue yesterday's broken journey west. It is the only section of the route, even in Thomas time, without a pub on the route.

***

Sparsholt

The nearly two-mile diversion to Sparsholt seems unplanned, then a further two miles to return to the Ridgeway this morning. Though Thomas had travelled some twenty miles from Streatley yesterday, a respectable distance, there is the sense that fatigue and perhaps more, was setting in. Had he continued to his stopping point on this day, yesterday, it would have only required a further eight-mile walk, just under thirty miles in total and well within his usual walking range.

It was not until the children were at their mid-morning play that he made an attempt at a start. Considering that he had made a 5 am start on more than one occasion previously, this was late indeed. Further evidence of his fatigue maybe. As if to defer his return to the road even further, he began this day with a reverie. His progress through Sparsholt was arrested by the sound of a piano playing a tune familiar to him. Thomas had a particular liking for old Welsh folk tunes, maybe Caradocs Hunt is one that has been lost in the mist of time for I can find no reference to it. Scott's *"waken lords and ladies gay"* which he referenced as a similar tune, however, is well known. His claim that it was the *"princeliest"* of hunting songs is rather odd for one such as Caradoc, who is remembered for his kindness to animals. Inspired by the music, he conflated a colourful tale woven with a description of the various ways in which the tune might be interpreted, the pictures it might conjure in other people's imagination. It reads like a series of descriptions of popular pre-Raphaelite illustrations. It is as if we are back in the room over the pub in Watlington with its extensive wall hung gallery. Then he weaves another tale into the weft referencing the Lady of the Night. Part Selene, part Welsh mythology, part invention, part referencing his own depression that he attempted to bury under this journey.

"What darkness the plummet fathoms, what 'bottom of the monstrous world' it touches, is not to be understood."

He eventually continued along the B4507 then up Blowingstone Hill passing the Blowing Stone itself on his return to the Ridgeway.

"The Blowingstone is a block of brown, iron-like sarsen stone standing on end, and of such a height that a man can bend over and comfortably blow into the mouthpiece at the upper side."

It is the site of the next illustration, No. 38: *'The Blowingstone'*.

It is no longer possible to accurately reproduce the illustration. The tree it appeared to almost rest against has gone. Beyond the tree in the illustration is what appears to be a fence of the adjoining property, so the site of the illustration would appear to be behind the stone looking back towards the road. The garden to the adjacent cottage, behind the fence. Modern shrubs make access to that side of the stone impossible, so my photo is taken from the opposite direction, witness the position of the stone disk next to the stone, now less the chain in the illustration, is reversed.

There are several illustrations in this area, though not all fit neatly into the geography of Thomas narrative. So, I have included them where Thomas walk appears to have passed closest to them.

On this day, the next illustration is possibly on a section of the Way that Thomas did not traverse. The narrative suggests that on the previous day he headed down to Sparsholt on a track to the west of Hackpen Hill. This day he returned to the Way along the C Class road past the Blowing Stone. If this is correct, then he missed a mile and a half section of the Way that would have passed Sparsholt Down. This is the site of the next illustration; No. 39: *'The Ridgeway near Blowingstone Hill Berks'*.

It looks back towards the east along the track towards Sparsholt Downs. The wide trackway that once traversed this eminence, like in so many other parts of the Way, has now been managed into a single rather than multi trackway. And entombed by trees into the bargain.

There is nothing in the narrative to suggest that Thomas ventured on to the roads to the north of Uffington Castle where some of Collins illustrations are sited but it is hard to believe he did not. If not on this journey, then on one of his previous visits to this area.

The Way rises to some 840 feet as it passes the White Horse and Uffington Castle, from this virtually flat turf tabletop it commands a 360-degree panorama.

"...I could see the Quarley Hill range and far over the Lambourn Downs to Martinsell Hill by Savernake; I could see Barbury Castle and the wooded hills of Clyffe and Wroughton, and Badbury, the Cotswolds, the Oxfordshire hills, Sinodun, and the Chilterns."

The location of the next illustration is more straight forward but not the illustration itself, No 40: 'Under White Horse Hill'.

It is on the north-facing hillside next to the White Horse.

I stumbled about in the long grass on this hillside to gain the location of the view in the illustration. The road curving around the foot of the hill shown in the illustration is unmistakable but the elevation required to match the extent of this road visible in the illustration I could not find. I suspect that once again Collins has introduced some artistic licence in order to make something more of the view. Either that or he has used the Edwardian drone again.

The narrative continues west, past Uffington Castle to Wayland's Smithy. A site he has already visited in one of his reveries becomes physically manifest. The location of the next illustration, No. 41: *'Wayland's Smithy'*.

It has been restored since Thomas passed this way, I say restored. Stones have been re-erected creating a new façade to the structure. I say new

175

because who really knows what it looked like in Neolithic times. What Thomas saw was a time-worn monument to an earlier age. What we have now is antiquarian conjecture and as Thomas said elsewhere, conjecture – *".... usually kept sternly in obedience to speculation".*

There was a chap sitting by a tree with his rucksack, taking an interest as I took my photo with my camera in one hand, trying to line up it up with the illustration I had in the other. I showed him the illustration I was using. He thought that the Smithy had been 'restored' into its present form in the 1920s. He suggested I sit on the stone at the foot of the entrance with my back to another to see if I could sense anything. I am not particularly sensitive, not a sceptic either but an action like this, undertaken with intention, focuses the consciousness.

We chatted while his partner explored the monument. It transpired that he had been ordained but over the years had begun to question the usefulness of modern religious orthodoxy. As he began to understand how deeply embedded pagan beliefs were in the early church, he had become drawn closer to both, eventually concluding that he had no option but to resign his ministry. This is, however, not a simple matter of choice. In order to release himself from his vows, he was required by the church to attend a retreat. He met others at the retreat that spoke wisely and in particular a monk, who he said came as close as anyone he had met to Merlin. It is natural to imagine that such a retreat was intended to recapture him for the church or at least to inform him of the error of his ways but the presence of such wisdom suggests that instead, the church was keen to help him safely and usefully on his way. It reveals an esoteric side of the church's ministry that few get to experience.

He now spends some of his time exploring ancient monuments. He had recently been to Avebury, which he believed is usually illustrated the wrong way up. That is, with north to the top of the page. In ancient cultures, the primary cardinal direction is usually to the south. Where the sun is in the northern hemisphere. Seen in this orientation, Avebury appears to represent a womb, the ceremonial avenues representing the fallopian tubes. Inside the outer circle are two smaller circles. He believed it was a representation of the triple goddess; a central part of the pagan belief system. The outer circle represents the womb or Mother and the two inner circles the Maiden and the Crone.

The Mother gives birth to the Maiden who already carries the eggs for the next generation. In this way three generations, Maiden, Mother and Crone are always linked in a triad. This is both biology and belief and a knowledge that he was sure was explicitly understood and celebrated in ancient times.

Having reached 840 feet by Uffington Castle, the Way wavered between about 650 and 700 feet on the stretch to Wayland's Smithy from which point it hovered at around 600-700 feet as far as its junction with Ermin Street near Liddington. Looking back along the Downs to Streatley Thomas reflected:

"The hills between Streatley and Liddington form a curve in the shape of a bow, a doubly curved Cupid's bow. Following this line, always keeping at the edge of the steep northward slope and surveying the valley, the Ridgeway carries the traveller for thirty miles as if along the battlements of a castle. He begins at Streatley by having the early morning sun of spring over his right shoulder; the full light of midday is on his left as he passes Letcombe Castle; the sun is going down on his right hand as he descends to

Totterdown and the pass for the Roman road and modem traffic between the hills."

Further evidence that he considered it to be ceremonially, a single days walk, not the two it took him.

At this point, the road had descended to just over 600 feet. Now it is not only the Roman Road that takes advantage of this gap in the downs but the M4 too. Thomas referred to the Shepherds Rest which presided over this crossroad; it is now an Indian. This might well have been where he stayed that evening for, he seems to ruminate on the authenticity of the Ridgeway beyond that point without travelling along it. The illustrator, however, does venture a little further.

Crossing over Wanborough Plain, the M4, then into one of the fields to the right of the road he found the site of the next illustration, No. 42: *'Under Liddington Hill Witshire'*. No longer a likely place for a shepherd and flock.

"The flocks no longer feed much on the hills, and, except when folded in squares of turnips or mustard, are seldom seen there. They have become more and more a kind of living machinery for turning vegetables into mutton, and only in their lambhood or motherhood are they obviously of a

different tribe from sausage-machines"

Thomas wraps up the last few miles of the Way quickly adding his conjecture to its provenance and speculating that the Way may have continued to Salisbury Plain, perhaps as far as the Dorset Coast but:

"beyond Wanborough there is so far no sufficient evidence for tracing the course of the Icknield Way...The two roads [Ridgeway and Icknield Way] came very near to one another in that parish; they may even have touched before the Ridgeway returned to its own place high up; and it is possible that as the Ridgeway in Berkshire has been mistakenly called the Icknield Way, so the lower part of what is now called the Ridgeway in Wiltshire may be the Icknield Way."

CHAPTER 9
NINTH DAY — STREATLEY TO EAST HENDRED BY UPTON AND HAGBOURNE HILL FARM

A brief description of the route:

About 11 miles. Thomas followed what was then and still is, the main road network that skirts the lowland edge of the downs. It was a short journey, perhaps he was troubled by fatigue for he certainly reached a still greater depth by the end of this day.

***

Streatley

Thomas began considering the provenance of the Icknield Way and the possible route of a connection between the Icknield Way in Oxfordshire and the Icknield Way in Berkshire. He reasoned, without drawing a firm conclusion that if a connection existed then it should either pass through Streatley or at one of the other nearby crossing points of the Thames. Possibly from Ipsden via South Stoke Ferry.

Streatley is the site of the next coloured illustration; 'Streatley Mill and

Church'. It is a view to the north from the approximate location of the ferry crossing that once plied the river between Streatley and Ferry Lane in Goring.

STREATLEY MILL AND CHURCH.

Such a view is no longer in the public domain. The entire Streatley riverside has been privatised in the past hundred years. Large houses now occupy the site of the former mill. The nearest I could get to a view of the church tower and a glancing one at that from a different orientation, was along Vicarage Lane through a gap in the trees.

Thomas headed north out of Streatley on the A329, the same road that had taken him up to the Ridgeway the day before but at the point where the Ridgeway peeled off to the west, he took the right-hand folk to the north on the A417 towards Moulsford Downs.

To the right are views across the open plain of the Thames Valley and to the left, the coombs at the foot of the downs. A little before Moulsford Bottom, the next illustration comes into view, No. 43: *'Moulsford Bottom'*.

The site of this illustration looks west towards Unhill Wood from the A417 about 2 miles out of Streatley, near Starveal Farm. The view is now well hidden from the road, so my photo is taken from a gap in the hedgerow next to a direction sign.

The Way rises slowly and uneventfully past the Aston's, Tirrold and Upthorpe in the north. They are no more than half a mile away but hidden from view. On the next stretch of road towards Blewbury, unusually, even today the road is remarkably free of hedgerow in stretches and affords a clear view across the immediate landscape both sides of the road with the scarp edge of the downs dominant on the left and later, the open hedgeless arable plain surrounding the ancient earthwork of Blewburton Hill which Thomas had passed close by on day six .

Blewbury Hill reaches nearly 300 feet on the section of the A417 that

185

Thomas followed before dipping down again towards the village. It is from this high point that the next illustration is sited, No. 44: 'Blewbury'. It is a view from the side of the A417 looking west towards Blewbury.

The village has only crept a field or two closer to the site of the illustration in the past hundred years but has become much more deeply cloaked in a blanket of trees

Blewbury.

On the edge of Blewbury Thomas passed the Barley Mow pub again, retracing his steps of day six. It was raining once more and this time he sought shelter in the deep overhanging eaves of a thatched building. Here he studied his map seeking a route beyond Upton that would take him off this *"unadventurous, level, probably commercial, road"*

UPTON.

Upton

Upton was just over a mile further along the A417, the road continued to decline little by little. Thomas was looking for a road that kept to the higher ground, aware that any road on low ground was unlikely to be the Icknield Way. He identified a route leaving Upton to the west beyond the railway towards Lollingdon Farm. As he headed towards the Didcot Newbury and Southampton Railway Thomas would have passed the George and Dragon, the possible site of the next coloured illustration; *'Upton'*.

The old map shows that the road on the approach to the pub has been significantly reengineered since Thomas passed this way and the buildings are no longer thatched. It seems to be a view along the A417 looking north but to me, it is not wholly convincing. I spent a considerable amount of time surveying the lanes within the village itself but did not manage to find a location any more convincing than this one. Though there is nothing in Thomas narrative to suggest that he ventured into the village, Collins illustrations show that he occasionally ventured off route. The village is much changed. What was a hamlet immersed in orchards is now yet another small village immersed in bungalows.

He passed the George and Dragon, crossed over the now abandoned railway and took the lane heading due west. This, now blacktop road, rises gently as far as the Chilton to West Hagbourne Road on Hagbourne Hill. From here it continues as a single carriageway road past Hagbournehill Farm offering clear views of Didcot power station to the distant right.

It is the site of the next illustration, No.45: *'Ickleton Meer, Hagbourne Hill near Upton Berks'*

The illustration is on a deeply rutted track on the approach to Hagbourne Hill Farm. The farm buildings were derelict when Thomas passed this way. They have been demolished since that time and replaced with new buildings on the same site.

A little beyond the farm, the A34 dual carriageway now crosses this landscape passing under the Way. Less than a mile further on, the Way crosses what is now the A4185 and what were then the open fields of Downs Farm. It is now the site of the Harwell Science and Innovation Campus. It is an alien in this agrarian landscape. The Way is arrow straight and flat, passing through large unhedged fields. The absence of higher ground beyond lends it an almost edge of the world look through all of the available 360 degrees. Harwell remains almost invisible on this approach to the A4185, though a line of trees teases with a slow reveal on the western horizon directly ahead. Then, suddenly everything changes. Immediately on the other side of the road we are in a suburban landscape of 'Drives and Avenues' and Pelican Crossings. The trees that appeared on the approach, as we get closer become not wild nature but the self-conscious plantings of a parkland landscape. The Pelican Crossing marks the portal through which we pass into it, past the Harwell day nursery then just as suddenly, back into the countryside again. An aberration that vanishes as quickly as it intruded into the journey. A figment of someone's suburban imagination briefly manifest.

Beyond, the Way reverts to a footpath. At Aldfield Common, Thomas encountered a gap of some hundred yards in the line of the Way but this missing section of track has since been formally established, perhaps by a suburban, tidy minded soul.

It seemed to have been raining for much of Thomas day and dispirited, he went off route again and completed the day in East Hendred only some 10 miles beyond his starting point in Streatley:

"As I had had as much rain as I wanted on my skin, I turned downhill under a long train of Lombardy poplars and very lanky ash trees into East Hendred for the night."

East Hendred

Thomas describes East Hendred as a *"thatched village built on the slopes of a little valley"*. The main street into the village appears deeply eroded with the cottages standing in parts, well over two metres above the road with steps connecting the two levels. This is the site of the next illustration, No. 46: *'East Hendred'*.

Approaching from the south along Newbury Road, it looks north towards the village centre. Once again, Collins appears to have found a site for his illustration some three metres higher than any I could find in the modern village. All but the cottage nearest the viewpoint have lost their thatch. Those in the middle of the photo now have the upper floor windows reconstructed as dormers.

Thomas retired to an inn.

The old map shows the Eyston Arms and the Plough Inn. Both were still trading until recent times. The Plough closed in 2017. It seems to have undergone a major refurbishment between 2009 and 2016 which exposed the previously hidden timber frame construction externally. It closed soon after and has been converted to residential use.

Wheatsheaf, East Hendred.

There is also a Wheatsheaf, it was not shown on the old map but still trades. Thomas gives no clue to his overnight stop but wherever it was, he struck up a conversation about the Way with a local and goes on to recommend to the reader the dull but accurate record of country life written in the books of Miss Eleanor G Hayden, who had lived in East Hendred, bemoaning how:

"So many books are written by bungalow countrymen that we have got used to pretty things, surprising things, pathetic things, country equivalents of the music-halls and museums of towns."

If Thomas stayed in any of these pubs it was likely to be this one, it's the only one he did not mention. It is a diminutive timber-framed building with a plain tiled roof that sits discretely in a corner of the village rather grandly called 'Chapel Square'. Inside, all the tables are set out for dinners. That's far from unusual today though it still seems incongruous in a pub like this. Standing next to the tiny bar, which is only offering Abingdon Bridge to non-wine drinkers are two aged locals. There is nowhere else for them if they just want a drink. It is not what Thomas would have recognised as a pub, perhaps it is not pretending to be one.

It had been raining much of the day. It is not clear if he cut his journey short or if this was a planned stopping point. Maybe he had genuinely become so dispirited and frustrated with the inclement weather that it formed the subject of his end of day reverie. He began by describing the impact of the rain almost light-heartedly but it did not stop there. In his now familiar, clever way, the reader is drawn in, involuntarily:

"Long I lay still under the sentence, listening to the rain, and then at last listening to words which seemed to be spoken by a ghostly double beside me. He was muttering..."

ever deeper into the reverie:

"The summer is gone, and never can it return. There will never be any summer any more, and I am weary of everything. I stay because I am too weak to go. I crawl on because it is easier than to stop."

and to its bleak conclusion:

"Blessed are the dead that the rain rains on."

Thomas Dark Night of the Soul. There is no evidence that Thomas emerged from this experience enlightened.

It is well known that Thomas was encouraged by Robert Frost to use 'In Pursuit of Spring' as a springboard, an inspiration for his first serious attempts at poetry. It is clear that he also went back to this work too and this passage in particular. Rain became the metaphor for depression in more than one of his poems. The passage in 'The Icknield Way', played out in this pub, is the long form.

∼

CHAPTER 10
TENTH DAY — EAST HENDRED TO WANBOROUGH BY LOCKINGE PARK, WANTAGE, ASHBURY AND BISHOPSTONE

A brief description of the route:

About 20 miles. Thomas continued on the roads and trackways skirting the edge of a wild and tempestuous downland landscape to the edge of Swindon.

***

East Hendred

Continuing west along a series of tracks and paths through rolling lowland countryside Thomas crossed the West Hendred road and Ginge Brook in quick succession. His westward progress was halted abruptly at Lockinge Park. The large country house that Thomas passed *"with some conservatories, elms, lawns, and water garden"* is no more but the diversion to the south around its grounds remains. Thomas re-joined what he conjectured to be the continuation of the original way in the very neatly manicured, proprietorial estate style cottages of East Lockinge and took a left turn past:

"...the good house of West Lockinge Farm, its barn and sheds and lodges gathered about it on one side of the road, and its ricks and elm trees opposite. The road was half farm-yard and half road and littered with

224

straw' and husks, where the fowls were stalking and pecking with a laziness that seemed perfectly suited to a Sunday early morning following a blazing harvest Saturday."

The farm is now distinctly to one side of the road. What appeared on the old map as a number of outlaying farm buildings on the right-hand side of the track, giving the sense that the road passed through the farmyard, have been demolished. The road turned north beyond the farm then quickly west again. From here, Thomas continued along a track running west past Round Hill until it reached a C Class road heading north into the outskirts of Wantage.

Thomas passed the Lord Nelson on the junction with the A417, it still trades. It was then an almost wayside pub surrounded by orchards according to the old map and is now surrounded by the familiar suburban markers of mini-roundabouts, pedestrian crossings and semi-detached houses. Thomas paused to comment on the pub sign.

"I recognized it as the work of that venerable artist who designs the faces of guys and turnip-men all over the country. I could tell that the man upon the signboard was Nelson because the uniform corresponded to the name painted below. The face was as much like Nelson as King George III, and it was entirely different from that on the other side of the board."

His view was that such a sign, however crudely or naively it attempted to portray a hero, was preferable to something taken from a history book or from an advert *"for somebody's food or embrocation"*. He continues this line of thought referring to the sign for the Coach and Horses which he considered *"...painful to see"*. There was a Coach and Horses in Wantage at one time. It was in Wallingford Street and maybe the pub he was referring to. If so, it is a rare indication that Thomas wandered off the route of the narrative followed in the book. In fact, he could either have taken Ormond Street, the more obvious continuation of the Way to the south of the town centre or followed Wallingford Road into it as far as the marketplace. This route would have taken him past Wantage Brewery and many pubs. Few are left. The Lost Pubs Archive currently lists 27 closed pubs in Wantage.

Wantage

I followed what may have been Thomas route into the town centre. I'm breaking one of his rules and admitting that I stayed here overnight here in the Bear Hotel, an old coaching inn.

The Bear Hotel, Wantage.

[Arkells 3Bs, Gold and Directors]

An impressive Georgian fronted building concealing its 16th Century origins. The original coaching courtyard has been enclosed serving as a restaurant space come circulation area that connects all the internal spaces on the ground floor. This is where all the modernising glamour has been concentrated. I ate in the courtyard, the derivative menu typical of this kind of establishment but for me at least, none the worst for that. Posh does not sit well with me. I drink beer with my meal, not wine and this kind of fare is enough for me to feel treated. In fact, I can feel treated in any of the 3-star hotel chains that have populated the English countryside in the past thirty years or so. Breakfast is in a first-floor function room with echoes of the grandeur of previous generations of the building. I sat next to an open window looking over the marketplace and the statue of Wantage's famous son, Alfred, contentedly watching the world pass by below.

Thoughts of the change in the past hundred years begin to crowd in. It seems unlikely Thomas would have stayed here but he might have popped in for refreshment, how different his experience of this town would have been.

The old map indicates the site of the breweries and many of the pubs trading in 1911. It also indicates the Town Hall, County Council Offices, the Corn Exchange, schools, mills, maltings, ironworks, smithy's, banks, chapels, churches and the railway station all in the compact commercial core of the town that had probably changed little over the course of a number of generations. This compact commercial core would also have included shops, merchants, professional offices of all kinds as well as dwellings. It suggests a compact civic life in which the butcher, the baker and the candlestick maker knew and interacted with each other commercially and socially. Another age. How easy it is to construct a romantic picture of the past through the selective presentation of the sediments of a previous age and create a history that never existed. This is what passes as popular modern history today. A bungalow and music hall history sanitised and made to look appealing with an admission charge at the entrance and a shop at the exit.

Wantage is a place that still retains the basic structure of its commercial core and even though it has been hollowed out, it is possible, just, to imagine the dynamic of that other age. An age that at best, Thomas caught only the tail end of. The dispersal of residents away from the relative economic self-sufficiency of a market town into the suburbs, the incursion of a new generation of corporate commercial businesses, the dominance of national brand names and the need to import merchandise from centres of mass production had already begun to take a firm hold by 1911.

The hard won social reforms that had begun in the nineteenth century and early twentieth century were propelled forward by the settlements following the great depression and the two world wars and led to a very English form of social democracy that gestated in London in the thirties. It spread across the rest of the nation in the brief 'new age' of the post-war years. Though the NHS is still regarded as its jewel in the crown there was so much more. The National Assistance Act, the National Insurance Act, National Health Service Act and the Legal Aid and Advice Act forming the four pillars of the Welfare State. It is often overlooked that the White Papers that precipitated these reforms were signed off in the war years by Churchill as well as Atlee. They were supplemented by the Education Act, the New Towns and the great raft of public ownership of the utilities and transport. Churchill of course soon about-faced and spitefully blitzed the Festival of Britain site at the first opportunity. As the euphoria of the early post-war years ran out of steam, the public estate has been incrementally sacked by the selectively misanthropic vandals of an older orthodoxy that Thomas would recognise from Coldiston.

As Thomas feared, Samantha and Gerry may believe they have swapped city life for country life but they have only swapped it for a suburban one. This is now a suburban country and in the wake of the post-war euphoria, and despite the rhetoric, one lead by governments with only suburban aspirations.

~

Whichever route Thomas took, around or through the town centre, he would then have followed the Port Way leading into Ickleton Road beyond it and the site of the next illustration, No. 47: *'Port Way Wantage'*.

It is taken along Port Way looking back towards the east from just beyond the junction with Locks Lane. King Alfred Grammar School, now an academy, features on the left-hand side of the image. A classic edge of town centre street graced by majestic elms which articulate and give a presence to the school buildings, rather than dominating them. This context is now lost. Only the pavements, road markings and traffic stand out in the modern image. It could be the result of the poor quality of my photographic skills but the buildings have become little more than an inconsequential backdrop to a traffic route.

The narrow B4507 leaves Wantage in a chasm of roadside trees, shrubs and hollow ways. It breaks free eventually near East Challow where the line of the downs dominates the landscape to the left. The road continues to snake across the land named by the old map as the Icknield Way, Ickleton Way and Roman Road at various points.

Unconvinced, Thomas looked for some sign of an alternative route avoiding *"Roman Way"* and took a left hand turning along a C Class road at Windmill Hill then a right along what is still a track as far as the B4001 Childrey Road. Unable to find any evidence of an earlier route, he returned to the B4507 on the approach to Childrey. In patches, the surrounding landscape opens up in the gaps in the roadside verdure, to the left towards the downs, at another, to the right across the Vale of the White Horse.

"The trees of Lisle Park gave lines of handsome beeches to either side of the road, trees of less than a hundred years, all well-shaped and, in fact, almost uniform, and planted at reasonable intervals."

A further hundred years on, each side of the road is indistinguishable from any other part of the road. The formal parkland landscape Thomas describes has faded away.

From here the Way is heavily marked by the topography it passes through, wrapping around a deep coombe then becoming distorted as the wildness of Dragon Hill presses in on the edge of the road. It then subsides into a temporary calm before the downs rush in again and the road is again distorted by the coombe which houses the Manger below Uffington Castle. Then suddenly, these wild energies are gone and the road follows evenly along the 150-metre contour as far as Ashbury.

In this dramatic section of road are two further illustrations. The first is No. 48: *'Dragon Hill'*.

"...an isolated eminence shaped like the butt of an oak tree..."

It is a view taken above the road, the trees lining the road appear along the bottom of the frame. Britchcome Farm sits nestled in a cleft.

Both the farm and the Dragon are now screened from view in this location. The Dragons tail can just about be decerned in a notch along the treeline to the centre-right of the photo.

An approximation of the illustration eventually comes into view beyond the farm.

The next illustration, No. 49: *'White Horse Hill'* is a little further along the road in the coombe looking up to the Manger with the White Horse just visible on the crest of the hill.

A rare, almost unchanged view a hundred years later.

For all the attractiveness of the early section of the Chilterns, the confluence of landforms in this section of the downs, the deep distorting folds in the landscape seem to be building to a crescendo that reaches its climax here, at the White Horse. The road may well rush us past this landscape today, preoccupied with other thoughts. That, in another age, this landscape became such a defining focus of cultural and spiritual life is a dynamic largely lost on us. Nice place for a picnic and a game of Frisbee for us bungalow pilgrims.

Ashbury

"Ashbury was the first village traversed by the road since Upton."

That is ignoring the small matter of Wantage. But of course, if he is being precise, Wantage is not a village.

As Thomas reached Ashbury, he speculated on a possible alternative route, a track running parallel to the main road leading from the church to Idstone, a feature he called the Green Terrace. It is the subject of the next illustration, No. 50: *'Green Terrace near Ashbury'*.

It is clearly marked on the old map as a bank like gradient but is marked on modern maps as nothing more than a footpath. The trees that have grown upon this feature now obscure its form. Collins was able to compose his view from the top of the embankment. A footpath still follows the line of the embankment but it is on the other side of the new treeline from where the view of the edge of the embankment is completely obscured. My photo is taken from a lower field to the right of the new tree line.

Ashbury is only a little changed, in size at least, since Thomas passed through. A new housing estate has been developed on an area next to the old mill buildings. A rather loose, brick and render suburban addition to the tight stone and thatch centre of the old village.

Thomas mentions the Rose and Crown which still trades but took refreshment elsewhere.

"I stopped for a little time at Ashbury, and asking for tea at a cottage and shop combined, I was asked into a silent but formidable Sunday assembly of three incompatible and hostile but respectful generations: a severe but cheerful grandmother in black and spectacles with one finger still marking a place in the Bible; a preoccupied, morose mother, also in black; a depressed but giddy daughter fresh from the counter of a London shop, and already wondering what she was going to do at Ashbury."

It was a Sunday in a village in which some at least, strictly observed the sabbath. Attempting to purchase some apples, Thomas was told in no uncertain terms that none were available and as if in observance of the Lords rules, even the trees themselves would withhold their harvest on the branches until Monday. He returned to the Teashop where he discovered:

"...that Sunday's tea cost twice as much as Saturday's or Monday's — it being apparently the right of the righteous to prey upon the damned...I hastened away, glad to have made these discoveries in the natural history of Ashbury."

Ashbury is the site of the next colour illustration; *'Ashbury'*. It is sited outside the Rose and Crown looking east.

The three cottages on the extreme right of the frame have been demolished and are now the site of a modern suburban detached house, a bus stop and the car park to the pub. If you squint your eyes, little else has changed but taking into account the parked cars, road markings and a firmer, straighter edge to the kerbstones it is only approximately the same place despite the extensive thatch.

ASHBURY.

The old tea shop could have been housed in the double bay windowed building with the look of a shop about it at the far end of the street. According to the old map, there was a garden next door, a suitable site for an apple tree. In fact, the illustration shows what could be a standard apple tree beyond the shop. Perhaps, more in tune with Thomas sensibilities on the day, maybe the tea shop was housed in one of the demolished cottages next to the bus stop.

207

Still an ideal premises for a tea shop.

Rose and Crown, Ashby

[Arkell's 3b's and Wiltshire Gold]

A gastro type pub but without overdoing it, most tables have condiments though not all have napkins and cutlery. The old teashop might have gone but the recent development has brought with it a new shop and tearoom. In observance of Asbury's traditions, it is not open on a Sunday.

I take a seat outside the pub, warm but shaded from the sun in a beer garden with an unexpectedly urban feel. Hard landscape and potted plants giving touches of lushness. The relaxing, soft dappled light from the sun encourages my mind to wander as I relax back into my chair.

In the early chapters of the book, Thomas differentiates the idea of a road from a destination. The road is the mechanism through which the process of travel can be realised, rather than the route to somewhere in particular. It is less where he will end up, more what effect, what change might be wrought by experiencing this process, this *"expensive medicine"*. So much of Thomas journey is no more than a description of the passing scenery, the flowers, the trees, the birds, the roadway surfaces and borders, the choice of routes and sometimes the pubs. It is well known that Thomas was a great walker, sometimes in company, sometimes as a desperate act of flight from his demons. He could lose himself to the world for hours, sometimes much longer. For all that, there is little or nothing in this to work to suggest he experienced any kind of healing from this process. It is only in the diatribes, the moments of reflection, the consequential encounters that any insight into his searching can be gained. None offer any resolution to his melancholy. The reconciliation and relief he found at the end of his life after enlisting, becoming a proficient map reader and finally being posted to a forward observer post in the front line in Arras confirm against all expectation that nature for him, proved not to be the cure. In some respects, the Icknield Way was a study of the distance between himself and the world he wished to live in.

~

Bishopstone

The road swept around Idstone and on to Bishopstone crossing the Wiltshire Berks border on the way. Here again, the Way was contorted as it passed through the village. Thomas would have passed in sight of the True Heart pub and rather further away, the Royal Oak. The True Heart closed in 2009.

"But the coombe and the bare Downs about it were so shaped by nature, by wearing, and apparently by deliberate but inexplicable cutting, that a mere road could not be traced with certainty."

This was the site of the last illustration and perhaps the most intriguing, No. 51: *'Coombe at Bishopstone'*

In the foreground is a thatched cottage with its roof virtually at road level, beyond the seemingly deliberately scalloped edge of the coombe, then in the distance the so called 'strip lynchets' high up on the top of the coombe. Modern verdure has obscured much of this view but even the illustration in Thomas book does not reveal all.

Hidden at the edge of the coombe next to an old mill pond and watercress beds, neighbouring the thatch cottage is 'The City', a veritable grotto of thatched waterside cottages that can only really be seen at their best by following the footpath from Hockerbench that weaves amongst them. It is like coming upon an echo of Elysium. A place hidden from the profane world. A place where the gods chosen, live out their blessed existence discretely. I exaggerate only slightly the sense walking into this unexpected place. It is as though the influence of the White Horses' magic is extending at least this far. There is more.

Though modern maps call the hillside sculpture 'strip lynchets', Thomas did not. Looking at their form in the landscape in this dramatic coombe, the idea that they were simply meant for growing cabbages is preposterous. Something else was at work here, something our bungalow country intelligence can no longer fathom. At the very least it is a deliberate sculptural intervention into the already naturally dramatic landscape that underlies it for purposes our aesthetic sensibilities can at least identify with, if not our reason.

Heading west again Thomas route is next diverted south around Hinton Parva rising gently up and down across the outliers to the downs and on the approach to Wanborough, glimpses of the landscape to the right open up fleetingly between the trees to reveal the very distant Cotswolds on the horizon. Just before Thomas route crosses Ermin Way he passes the Black Horse beer house. An Arkell's pub that closed in 2012.

Wanborough

Beyond Ermine Way Thomas entered Wanborough, then a loose scatter of buildings spread between Lower Wanborough in the north and Upper Wanborough to the south-west. It has since been consolidated with post-war development between the two leaving Upper Wanborough as the satellite of the main settlement. Thomas route took him into Upper Wanborough and a fork in the road where he passed what he called the Calley Arms. It still trades as the New Calley Arms.

C aley Arms, Wanborough.

[Tribute, Doombar, Prescott Ales Hill Climb]

A domestic scaled building with a very homely feel inside. This might not be the same building that Thomas knew as the Calley Arms but it has something of the feel of a beerhouse of that age about it.

Reflecting on the downs at Bishopstone and the carved *"green terraces like staircases"*, Thomas paused to consider the relationship between art and landscape.

"Sheep were strewn over some of these terraces, making arrangements of white dots of a fascinating irregularity. Unless it has become a trick, only a great artist could make similar arrangements of equal beauty. The unknown laws which produce these inevitable accidents are great managers of the beautiful."

Thomas insight is interesting. That there is a natural sort of ordering process at work in the natural world that produces beauty. A force working in nature as certain as gravity. A law indeed that orders the distribution of flowers, grasses, trees, hills, mountains and rivers and the sheep as they move about within the landscape. It can order our affairs too, as is obvious in so many landscapes in which we have played a part. It can be seen in the distribution of field boundaries, woods, planting belts, farms, and villages.

And make no mistake, in our more exalted moments, we can create beauty. Sometimes unselfconsciously, but also deliberately. Participation in this process comes naturally. In fact, to our own sensibilities, we can create beauty of an order that nature itself does not achieve when left to its own devices. This simple fact alone, our contribution to this process, gives substance to the importance of humanities place in the natural world for there is nothing else within it that has the capacity to accomplish this and our ability to appreciate beauty, validates it.

There are classic forms that do not appear naturally, an avenue of trees, a village pond, the church nestled in a fold in the landscape, the cottage garden through to the parkland landscapes of country houses, all are undertaken with varying degrees of intention and accomplishment.

Where we are in tune with this natural art, we see only harmony. Unlike the sheep that roam our fields, the gift of self-consciousness enables us to break free from the rules of the natural world. Sometimes it creates something astonishing and at others, the resulting ugliness stands out like a sin.

~

From here, Thomas took the Ham Road south then a right-hand fork towards Liddington because:

"...it seemed possible to connect it with one, very much like the Icknield Way and in a similar relation to the Downs, going south-westward through Wroughton and Broad Hinton, and from there either to Avebury or to Yatesbury, and so by Juggler's Lane to Cherhill on its way to Bath."

In fact, Thomas found little or no evidence of the Way, and in this area the maps, new or old had long since stopped referring to any of the roads by this name or any of its derivations.

"Liddington clump, the straight ridge and the "castle" rampart upon it, were clear ahead as I took this turning...."

It is now a road of an impossibly neat, linear suburban landscape of mown verges and clipped hedges with all the appearance of an executive enclave of Swindon.

Liddington

The large detached houses that now line Ham Road aside, Liddington has seen little development in the past hundred years apart from the B4192 that now threads its way through the village. As Thomas entered Liddington he passed the Bell, now trading as The Village Inn.

The Bell, Liddington.

[Arkells 3Bs, Wiltshire Gold, Hoperation IPA]

Another domestic scale Victorian building that is attempting to look older. It has a large dining room, attached in more recent times. A strangely old fashioned feel with the fake timber-framed and brick infill bar front and its conservative choice of furnishings. Darkwood pub furniture is today so ubiquitous that it can seem like the traditional form but it is anything but. There is only one description of a pub in this book, more in his other works. It is likely that Thomas would have been more familiar with the lighter, warmer tones of pine, oak and elm, fashioned into stools, settles and bodger crafted chairs or the walnut of The Four Elms, all worn silky smooth by generations of use.

The disjuncture between the world Thomas was living in and his attraction to the world it was replacing is perhaps more clearly stated in Pursuit. It can seem misplaced, luddite even, but his apparent sympathies for suffrage and social progress suggest that he was no reactionary. Nor was it nostalgia. What he was expressing was disquiet, a disquiet that something was being lost. This sense of loss goes rather deeper than the disappointment or the insecurity borne out of the demise of the familiar. For despite his affinity with the natural world, Thomas was no countryman. He was only familiar with country life by proxy. While it provided the resource material for much of his work, both prose and poetry, his relationship with it was not as one who's livelihood depended upon it but as one of the new leisured class. His expression of loss was a judgement.

Thomas was not a writer of manifestos but it is not hard to appreciate that at the heart of his disquiet were the changing values and social relationships with the natural world that had been playing out for a generation or more. What was being lost from the human consciousness and what was replacing it as the urbanisation of society advanced was something that had been expressed explicitly by the likes of Ruskin and Morris. I doubt that he necessarily agreed with these prophets of a previous generation wholeheartedly. However, his cynical asides, his characterisation of the bungalow and music hall consciousness, the dumbing down of the urban and suburban populations relationship with the countryside was no less insightful.

The great strides that were being made by science, technology and commerce were inclined to squeeze nature out of the culture that he was born into. At the height of empire, it could seem reasonable to assume that it was the rest of the world that needed to catch up, to be taught how to do it by their superiors. Through the absurd notion of British Exceptionalism, there was a belief in some quarters that Britain set the example to the rest of the world. Thomas was flowing against this tide of history to some extent. Now, given the projected changes to the climate that face us, it becomes clearer now than it was then that we cannot go on this way. No fantasy of exceptionalism will lead us through the looming hazards of the

Anthropocene.

~

Thomas left Liddington on an initially sunken road, south-west towards the diminutive hamlet of Badbury. Beyond the village, the modern road has been realigned and now bridges across the M4 which bisects the two settlements.

Badbury

The old map shows a beerhouse in Badbury now trading as the Bakers Arms.

Bakers Arms, Badbury.

[Arkell's 3B's, Wiltshire Gold]

Also furnished with traditional pub furniture but in a colour closer to elm than fake Victorian mahogany. That aside, the whole pub has a lighter and more modern feel with a boarded floor, albeit a look-alike laminate. Like so many modernised pubs it follows an aesthetic that would have been alien to Thomas, though none the worst for it. It is more informed by the present rather than hiding behind the folly and fake of an imagined tradition.

In its normal use, esoteric knowledge is seen as information that is held from general knowledge by a small cabal of people serving their own self-interest. By another measure, they are protecting it, maintaining its continuity through the generations until the day when the rest of humanity is at last worthy of this knowledge. There are other dynamics. Knowledge becomes occulted by self-assurance and the conceit of exceptionalism, our modern discoveries trump the ravings of the past, the less cultured, the less civilised..... the less British. Substitute any other nationalist trope if you are reading this overseas. With all these things in play, during the passage of time there are things that have been accidentally or conveniently forgotten, avoided or suppressed. By letting this happen, to coin a phrase, we cease to be 'good ancestors'. James Salk's notion of a Good Ancestor has become someone that buys funeral insurance and passes the good news on to a neighbour in a garden centre.

~

Beyond the pub, the road sweeps around to the west past a second post-war instalment of Badbury which, according to the old map, appears to have been overlayed on a farmstead or workshops. Continuing, Thomas crossed a Roman Road, now the A346 and continued into Chiseldon.

Chisledon

It was half-past five when he arrived and feeling hungry, Thomas sought an inn. At the first:

"On the opposite side of the road a small, quiet crowd of drinkers in black coats and hats waited to be let in at six. No one answered my knock."

This was the first of a series of refusals as Thomas attempted to find a bed for the night in both pubs and private houses.

"To be elbowed out at nightfall after a day's walking by an unconscious conspiracy of a whole village was enough to produce either a hate of Chisledon or a belief that the devil or a distinguished relative was organizing the opposition."

As he looked for accommodation for the night, the serial rejections pub by pub, house by house led him in the end to a pantomime, written as farce. A rare self-deprecating comedy. He had either given up on any serious hope of completing his mission to fathom the Way, or had became resigned at least, to his depression and the absurdity of his expectations.

Patriots Arms, Chisledon.

[London Pride, Doombar]

Smokehouse it is now. What kind of name for a pub is that. It is a name for a place that is no longer a pub. I recall a period in the late '60s and early '70s when there seemed to be a fashion for converting pubs into grill bars. As fashion moves on, the form dies away and yet another public house is converted into a private one.

By the time he reached here, Thomas had well and truly lost the Way. By the time I had reached here, I had lost Thomas.

The old map appears to show a compact partly industrial settlement. Chisledon with a station, small marshalling yard and a foundry. Something other than the termination of a great walk. Now it seems not even that. Just a dull dormitory on the edge of Swindon. Still anything but the termination of a great walk. How quickly the energies dissipate that for miles previously, seemed to be building, soaring towards the White Horse.

He speculated about the way continuing to Barbury Castle, Avebury, Bath or the Dorset Coast. He fantasized about it continuing to St David's but based on my experience of the journey, it culminated in the Vale of the White Horse via that pagan portal at the entrance to the Smithy.

We are on the edge of Swindon, an unglamorous town that plays the part of a punctuation to Thomas journey along the Icknield Way. For Thomas, it was a comer or maybe a semi-colon rather than a full stop. He had travelled through the magical landscape of the Ridgeway twice, touching the edge of what in more recent years has become crop circle country. If we suspend our tendency to regard the press as the source of informed opinion, put aside its presentation of this phenomenon and the idea that those making them are simply trying to ridicule the gullible, we will find instead that many of those that started in this way have been affected by what they have done. Whatever the original motivation might have been, however cynical, some confess that the ongoing impulse to persist with this activity year after year has become compelling. One reason they put forward is that they are making art in the landscape. They describe how the planning and development of a new design each year addresses an embedded need for creativity, how it can even seem to open a previously silent spiritual side of their nature. It would not be unreasonable to say that, as they enter the field and lay down the design, they are carrying out a ritual in the landscape. Those that visit these places and claim to 'feel the vibes' have not so much been gulled by pranksters but affected by the outworking of that ritual process. It could be said that these are temporary temples. Temples etched out on the landscape by an unintended ritual.

Such impulses go back to the dawn of time. History suggests that we are natural temple builders. Megaliths, stone circles, Wayland's Smithy, the White Horse, the so-called strip lynchets of Bishopstone....the parish church are all in this context, temples. None are placed into the landscape accidentally or in an arbitrary way, they interact directly with it and in some cases maintain a continuity of use that crosses many generations.

Alongside these deliberate interventions, there are also unselfconscious ones.

Just as Thomas observed how sheep became "artfully strewn across the terraces", how hedgerow and field boundaries can create a harmonious landscape without any self-conscious planning, Landscape Zodiacs could well be the manifestation of this same unselfconscious dynamic, the product of the outworking of our interaction with the natural world written, as it were, as a topographical script. From my limited knowledge of zodiacs, they are not exact representations of the zodiacal signs but areas of land defined by landscape features in which some correspondence with the sign has become evident. Some of these landscape features are natural, others man made, the signs themselves are a composite of both. A topographical feature, place name, a custom, the name given to a house by its keeper, an historical event, an ancient site... all these things. The site of a megalith, the site of a parish church are conscious creations. Zodiacs may simply be the product of the invisible ordering force to which Thomas alluded. To coin another phrase, as above, so below. Such a correspondence can seem improbable until one happens upon that rare zone – that transcendent sensation of the connection between all things, when the outworking of these dynamics can at once seem entirely plausible. Thomas experienced such moments of extra-sensory connection, they are expressed with a subtle clarity in his poetry and sometimes in his prose reveries, even in The Icknield Way.

Since the proposition of the Glastonbury Zodiac, many others have been proposed up and down the country in more recent years. I would speculate that there are probably many more than is currently proposed and perhaps, they blanket the entire landscape like an interlocking Escher pattern, just awaiting our attention.

Given that attention, what comes forward is a tool, a framework with which to look at the landscape on a wider scale, for making connections between things separated by time and apparent purpose, a way of interpreting our cumulative contribution to the natural world, a tool, even... to help us reaffirm our relationship with it by engaging our capacity for introspection. While this natural ability of introspection and interpretation seems to be inbuilt, it is not always embraced and is often denied.

The proposal of a landscape zodiac is normally preceded by conjecture and then research. The investigation and fieldwork which often reveal the associations between the place and the sign also seem to uncover our discrete presence. Whatever its 'official' history, the Icknield Way has come into focus as an *"entity"* across the past 300 - 400 years through the investigation and conjecture of generations of antiquarians. It is something that has been discovered, been given meaning and purpose through interpretation as much as it is something that has been self-consciously created like a stone circle. This process of discovery, conjecture and proposition is as much part of a ritual as the design and execution of a crop circle, the siting of a parish church or a standing stone. I would go further to say that it is the same for a housing estate, an office block, a nuclear power station, the compulsion to fell a rain forest or the gathering of a literary society to commemorate a writer's birthday by moving through a place familiar to him and reading from his works.

 All can be judged in terms of harmony or sin.

The use of the word ritual is of course both necessary and unfortunate, ladened as it is with unhelpful overtones. A ritual is just another word for a methodology to obtain a specific end. This unnatural division between the so called mystical and the mundane is no more than the division between the inner and outer worlds. Its use seems to switch off useful parts of the consciousness in those that reject the inner world and often, over excites those that don't.

Our participation in natural processes is reflected in everything. Its interpretation provides some tantalising evidence that our relationship with the natural world is dynamic rather than arbitrary or accidental and never innocent. A zodiac is just another place to ponder the nexus between man, nature and meaning.

Following Thomas along the Icknield Way has led me here, so would any of this have meant anything to Thomas. Almost certainly not in its raw form. Thomas was a cynic. His engagement with such things is absent in the kind of descriptive prose he produced to describe the landscape on this walk, but the significance of a loss of an intimate relationship with the countryside he would have understood, his connection seeps through so much of his more abstract, considered work in the diatribes, the fantasies, the prose and the poetry.

Walking can be meditative as Harry Hooton inferred when he described Thomas as a walking companion and reminisced how *'we just walked in healing silence'*. Thomas frequent visits to churches in both Pursuit and the Icknield Way can at first seem trivial diversions but the sheer number recorded in these books suggest that he was doing more than simply following habitual diversions from his route. This was clearly a major activity when he was out walking and probably indicates a much deeper undeclared need than an interest in regional surnames. More, an attempt to fathom meaning through the spent force of the lives of others by the manner in which they have been remembered by those that knew and loved them.

Whether he would have used landscape zodiacs as a tool of contemplation had the concept been available to him can only ever be an open question but his legacy is the evidence that he did use what tools were available to him to great effect. And, dare I say it, travelling from pub to pub and into inn yards drinking ale in the manner of Borrow in hope of meeting adventures.....would rank amongst those tools.

∼

EPILOGUE

D olau Cothi Arms, Pumpsaint.

I had always intended to follow Thomas here. The reason for undertaking this additional leg of the journey was amplified, to some extent, by the discovery of Lewis Edwards references to the Pumpsaint Zodiac following my initially rather incidental references to other landscape zodiacs in both Pursuit and this book. It seemed like a nice correspondence but little more, however, the weight of its meaning seemed to increase unexpectedly towards the end of my journey along the Icknield Way following Thomas remarks about the distribution of sheep on the Bishopstone hillside.

The sense of meaning was amplified further when I logged onto the Dolau Cothi Arms website to book a room. There on the website was yet another reference to the Pumpsaint Zodiac. It transpired that following on from Lewis Edwards original proposition, further studies had recently been undertaken into the Zodiac. Over a number of years, Jay Laville had been studying the Zodiac, both in the field and on maps and had published an interim report on this research entitled an 'Introduction to the Pumpsaint Temple of the Stars.

I drove to the pub heartened.

Sensing that I might have overshot the turning, there came a point along the A40 when I realised that I needed help to find the pub, set as it is, deep within a Welsh geography that was completely unfamiliar to me. I was still some miles away, so I fed the postcode into the satnav and let it take me where it would. In retrospect, I should have paid more attention to the route it took me along. As far as I can tell now, it took me off the A40 near Nantgaredig, north along the B4310 and through some glorious countryside. As I drove, I wondered what superlatives Thomas might have used to describe it. Today, we have a simple shorthand. 'The Shire'. After a few miles, the landscape began to open out, less homely, more drama as if echoing other parts of middle earth. Rohan came to mind. At Llansawel the road touched the B4337 before turning off onto a C Class road. There came a point when the road ahead became ringed by hills, each seeming the perfect place for a hill fort. A little further on, the satnav took me onto another C Class road heading north. It narrowed still further, blind bends and passing places only, snaking into ever tighter white knuckle coils until at last it opened out again and joined the A482 for the final run into Pumpsaint. The centre of Temple of the Stars, the Pumpsaint Zodiac.

Studying Jay Laville's book later, I discovered that this route had taken me along the belly of Canis Major, skimming along the shell of Cancer then skirting past Virgo and from Llansawell, winding round the paws and breast of Leo.

Relaxing back into the now open road, I began to wonder how on earth Thomas got here in the age before mass motorised transport. Not the way

I came, I presumed. In 1911 Lampeter was served by the railway, Llandeilo still is but how did he cover the final leg of his journey... and why. What possessed him to choose this place to pull his book together ready for publication, to write the dedication to Harry Hooton. Such thoughts were still circulating in my mind as I approached the pub.

Ah, maybe he cycled.

I had chosen the smallest room the pub had available thinking that maybe, taking into account Thomas usual preoccupation with thrift that punctuate his books, this is the one he would have chosen. It has diamond pattern casement windows set into a recess in the thickness of the stone walls which gives the impression of a bay window from the inside. I imagine a small desk in place of the central heating radiator that now occupies this space. It overlooks the road. The room has a lofty ceiling and now, an en-suite.

The curtesy tray is stocked with bottled water, tea, coffee, biscuits and remarkably, a decanter of port. This is entirely new to me.

I would like to say that I sensed his presence, but I did not. Maybe in the bar then.

I washed my evening meal down with three pints of Tenby Harbour Sea Bass topped up with a pint of Llanddarog from Coles Family Brewery. All five star but by the time I returned to my room I concluded, reluctantly, that the port was a step too far.

During the course of my meal, I was handed a copy of a local history book written by David TR Lewis entitled, 'Family Histories and Community life in North Carmarthenshire'. It contained a section on Pumpsaint and against my expectations, answered, to my mind at least, the reason why Thomas had come here. He had followed George Borrow who had stayed here in 1854:

"I entered the inn of the 'pump saint'. It was a comfortable old fashioned place with a very large kitchen and a small parlour. The people were very kind and attentive and soon set before me in the parlour a homely but

savoury supper and foaming tankard of ale. After supper I went into the kitchen and sitting down with the good folks in an immense chimney corner, listened to them talking in their Carmarthenshire dialect.... I arose about eight and went out to look about me. The village consists of little more than half a dozen houses... the inn is a good specimen of an ancient welsh hostelry. Its gable is to the road and to a little space on one side of the way. At a little distance up the road is a blacksmith's shop. The country around is interesting, on the north-west is a fine wooded hill – to the south a valley through which flows the Cothi, a fair river, the one whose murmur had come so pleasingly upon my ear in the depth of night." ....GB 1854.

For once, one hundred, one hundred and seventy years indeed, seems inconsequential.

Then I remembered....this was less a discovery, more forgetfulness for Thomas had referred to Borrow's visit in the dedication.

There remained one last thing to do. A final destination.

Eglwys Gadeiriol Tyddewi

Sitting in the pews of St Davids Cathedral, I cast my eye around the nave. The round arches of the Romanesque lower storey, the pointed arches of the second storey surmounted by the round arches of the clerestory, a bit of a mix. Then in the aisles, gothic windows with something of the Victorian Restoration about them. The nave ceiling, a stunning geometric timber structure coordinated with the bays of the nave arcade.

The young attendant tells me that the roof was constructed in the sixteenth century to replace the original stone vaulted roof that had become unstable. The evidence of a much steeper roof is clearly visible outside the building, impressed onto the west face of the tower. The roof of the side aisles was probably replaced at the same time. They reveal the modern conceit that things were always done so much better in 'the olden days' for here, there is no coordination with the aisle structure. The roof supports clash horribly and randomly with the aisle windows.

Thomas would not have been looking at the architecture but at the inscriptions left on behalf of the dead, seeking something he could make an irreverent comment about.

The modern open courtyard and timber-framed links to the refectory on the site of the cloisters, together with the steel and timber gallery that floats in the refectory space have been accomplished with far greater care, sensitivity, craftsmanship and success than the ceiling to the side aisles. The young attendant described the cathedral, and this is the case with most other cathedrals', as a broken jigsaw. Despite being assembled from several jigsaws, some parts sit harmoniously together, others do not and age is no measure of their success. We had the capacity for clumsiness and bodging five hundred years ago too.

I'm here in strange times. I am aware that including a reference like this to this book dates it, irrevocably. It is not something a professional writer would do, or at least, their editors might warn them away from it.

So it goes.

My visit to both Pumpsaint and St David's was delayed. I had intended to come here months ago but I was delayed by the Covid 19 outbreak. In fact, I finally made the trip a little after the first lockdown had begun to be lifted, aware that it was a small window of opportunity and if I did not do it then, at the end of August, then the reported statistics were telling me, despite government assurances at that time, that a second lockdown would soon preclude it. It is a leavening experience, our detachment from the natural world, its capacity for biting back against our missed steps as we put stress on it, be that wet markets, resource exploitation or the continuing encroachment into the habitats of other creatures. While history provides us with many examples of the ways in which nature can unleash a pestilence, we are now, irrespectively, in uncharted territory. From this viewpoint, the conclusion of all this is yet to be written. There are regular soft news items on the TV, interviews with members of the general public who have rediscovered community life in this crisis, better ways of living, a rebalancing of priorities and all willing the continuation of this enlightenment beyond the end of the crisis to a new dawn. As if that were possible. Nothing is more fragile than moments of soft reflection. The distraction of our minds inner rantings will inevitably ensure that we return to the well-worn track. Change. The inertia of vested interests that is set against such wishful thinking is overwhelming. Are we too simple to understand that we no longer own that right, the right to change, maybe we never have. I hope I'm wrong.

For the time being and who knows when it will change, travelling as I did at the start of this journey, travelling as Thomas did or Borrow or Belloc is on hold. There is a queue of people in face masks outside every pub in the city. Every pub that is open that is. The lucky ones, already sitting socially distanced on the tables outside probably had the foresight to book in advance. *"turning into an inn yard for the chance of drinking ale in the manner of Borrow"* is not an option. These are no longer public houses in the accepted sense and how many will survive. At their worst, a den of iniquity, at their best, more than just a focus of community life, an eye on the health of the community itself. At both extremes, woven into the very fabric of our culture and reflecting the best and the worst. The outside world suddenly seems so much smaller, more private. Their demise will remove yet one more reason to cross the threshold of our suburban sanctuaries and engage with the still living and breathing world beyond.

~

I'm Standing on the west coast, facing the Atlantic. It does not take too much of a leap of the imagination to plot the continuation of the Icknield Way from Pumpsaint, through St David's past Ramsey Island on the left and between the Bishop's Islands beyond to the Americas, to North of Boston specifically, the road Thomas chose not to travel.

To eulogise the poetry is one thing, to eulogise the man, quite another. Within the compass of his consciousness, he probably got as close to explaining reality to himself as anyone does but he had all humanities common flaws too, perhaps more than some. It is his melancholy that forces him to attempt to peel back the veils. Not everyone bothers. His poetry has left us with a legacy of art and insight into that nexus between man, nature and meaning that we are too capable of ignoring. His journeys into the natural environment were not to indulge the senses but to attempt to fathom the meaning of all this pain. That is the ongoing mission of all art, a road not taken by all but a road without end, a road that has diverse ends and as Thomas claimed, a road on which what is found along it, is likely to inform us of more than the destination.

Deep emersion into the countryside over several days is affecting. But sadly, Thomas is no example to us for though he spent more time deeply immersed in the countryside than most, it seemed to get him nowhere except to confirm the extraordinary unyielding nature of reality. What value does his journey have when it did not appear to provide the resolution or cure to his condition. Do the fragmentary insights yielded up along the way make the effort required to uncover them worthwhile. Can we realistically expect any more from such an expedition. By the time he reached Chisledon, I believe he had the answer to that. His next journey was less challenging, perhaps a little closer to his publisher's expectations and contained much less *"...of the mystery of the road about it."*

It is in the nature of an ephemeral route like the Icknield Way to have no certain beginning and many possible endings as Thomas speculated on the way to Swindon. There is nothing certain about the route of the Way, we can choose our own route and our own endings as others have before us. The gulf between gathering insights and finding answers is and will always remain unbridgeable. Without that paradox, there is no mystery of the road and little purpose in travelling.

Presumptuous as it may seem, I made this last leg of this journey for Thomas. This was the ending he could have conjured for his book had he been in better spirits.

OTHER BOOKS

Another Man in Pursuit of Spring

Revisiting Edward Thomas 1913 Cycle Ride from Wandsworth to Somerset

In March 1913, shortly before the outbreak of World War One, Edward Thomas cycled from Wandsworth in South London to Somerset - in search of spring.

The journey took Thomas across the soft underbelly of southern England, meandering through cities, towns, villages and hamlets - as well as open countryside - during a period of great change. He sought tangible evidence of the enduring countryside of his youth as well as the countryfolk that traditionally inhabited it.

However, Thomas was exposed to the inevitable auguries of change that were sweeping across the English countryside at that time. This book looks to retrace Edward Thomas journey through the English countryside, revisiting his loves, preoccupations and deeper concerns. In the process a more modern set of auguries place questions on the path to our own future.

Going Public

An ordinary life seen through the bottom of a beer glass in pubs that the writer
last visited twenty, thirty or even forty or more years ago.

Printed in Great Britain
by Amazon

16625742R00138